HELP 1 ™

Handbook of Exercises for Language Processing

Authors:
Andrea M. Lazzari
Patricia Myers Peters

Volume 1:
Auditory Discrimination
Question Comprehension
Association
Auditory Memory

LinguiSystems®

Skill Area:	Language
Interest Level:	1st grade thru Adult
Reading Level:	Non-readers thru 1.5

LinguiSystems, Inc.
3100 4th Avenue
East Moline, IL 61244

Printed in the U.S.A.
ISBN 1-55999-045-7

1-800-PRO IDEA
1-800-776-4332

About the Authors

Andrea M. Lazzari, Ed. D., is a private educational consultant in Richmond, Virginia. She has worked as a speech-language pathologist in the public schools, in a community clinic, and in private practice for a total of eight years. She has also been a teacher of preschool handicapped students and the Supervisor of Early Childhood Special Education Programs for the state of Virginia. In addition to co-authoring the *HELP* series for LinguiSystems, Andrea is also the author of *Just for Adults*.

Patricia Myers Peters, M. Ed., CCC is employed as a speech-language pathologist by Rehabilitation Services of Roanoke, Inc., Roanoke, Virginia. She works with a communicatively disordered population ranging from preschool through geriatric ages.

Andrea and Patricia have co-authored nine publications in the *HELP* series with LinguiSystems since 1980.

August 1991

Dedication

This book is respectfully dedicated to Russell Murphy and the Reverend Curtis Robertson.

Table of Contents

Introduction

This book has been written to help speech-language pathologists, teachers of the learning disabled, parents and other interested individuals in planning remediation activities for clients with auditory or language learning disabilities. This book originated from our frustration in trying to find materials in book or manual form which would provide the quality, variety and range of exercises needed in daily therapy with clients exhibiting varied deficits, abilities, and ages. We were seeking a book which did not require accompanying materials, was not a portion of an expensive kit, and could be used by para-professionals and parents, as well as by speech-language pathologists and teachers.

In presenting this handbook, we have attempted to provide a sufficient amount of material for repeated practice and drillwork, which is vital in the remediation of language deficits. In addition, we have included more difficult exercises to be used with older students and adults. These exercises have also been found to be helpful to post-stroke patients with deficits in auditory processing and verbal expression. All exercises contained within this handbook are or are similar to exercises we generated and implemented daily in our therapy sessions. The various exercises are intended to be used in individual or small group therapy sessions; however, they may also be successfully used in learning centers and self-contained classrooms.

Since *HELP* was first introduced in 1980, we have received overwhelming, enthusiastic response from our colleagues. Our initial goals to produce an inexpensive, practical and quality product apparently were met and appreciated by other professionals, parents and para-professionals in their work with language impaired individuals of all ages. Suggestions for improvement have been noted throughout the years and have been combined with some of our original ideas for the product to bring you the new, improved *HELP* manuals.

Individuals familiar with the original manuals will immediately recognize the new spiral binding designed to give each book greater durability and to aid in photocopying. Limited reproduction of the exercises is now permitted to facilitate the effective use of *HELP* in carryover activities outside the therapy situation. Answers for strictly auditory tasks are printed after the stimuli, as in the original version of *HELP*. The answers for sections to be presented as either visual or auditory tasks have been moved to an answer key section at the back of the manual. This change allows *HELP* to be presented as reading and visual tasks, and not just as auditory tasks.

The IEP goals have been retained and instructions have been added for those individuals utilizing the product in a visual mode. The client experiencing difficulty processing the material either acoustically or visually can benefit from the new format because the auditory + visual mode can more easily be utilized and either the auditory or the visual element can be gradually faded.

HELP is divided into logical chapters covering a broad range of activities. We have included those areas with which we have had the most success, hoping to provide a therapeutic instrument that is economical, practical, and thorough. Activities are provided at the end of each chapter to aid in carryover to everyday situations. The following guidelines are offered for effective utilization of the tasks in *HELP*.

1. Many tasks are presented as written worksheets for the client. Use your own judgment in presenting the tasks orally or as worksheets, depending on the ability of your client and your overall purpose for specific remediation.

2. As the ages and skills of the children or adults will vary, use your own judgment as to which portions of each section should be used for therapeutic sessions. An attempt has been made to rank the exercises, when possible, from the easier items to the more difficult.

3. Common, correct responses have been provided for almost all items in the answer key. There may, however, be other acceptable answers, depending on the client's experiences and cultural background. Again, use your discretion in determining correctness of responses.

4. Many repetitions of items may be necessary before target accuracy levels are reached. Accuracy rates should be kept on the specific items chosen to be within the client's range of ability.

5. Strive to achieve carryover of target concepts in conversation, everyday and classroom activities through constant repetition, questioning and stressing of specific concepts. These exercises may be used by parents and teachers' aides successfully with little explanation from the clinician. Communication between home and school is essential if carryover is to be effective. Auditory processing underlies all language reception, processing, and output. Carryover is essential to derive the maximum benefit from therapy.

The quality, variety and range of materials have not been changed in revising *HELP*. Some adjustments in stimulus items and answers have been made, however, to allow *HELP* to remain current. We hope that the improvements that have been made to the *HELP* manuals will satisfy some, if not all, of the needs expressed to us and to LinguiSystems over the years. Your support and constructive suggestions have been and will continue to be very much appreciated. We hope you will find *HELP* to be beneficial to you in your everyday therapy and instruction experiences.

January 1987   AML
                                                     PMP

Auditory Discrimination

Auditory discrimination, or the ability to perceive differences between auditory stimuli, provides for appropriate perception and encoding of verbal language. The inability to discriminate differences in similar phonemic elements in varied positions of the acoustic stimulus results in improper learning of vocabulary and a general disruption in the expansion of receptive language skills. Additional difficulties in sound/symbol association, as well as disruption in perceiving the presence or absence of sounds in various units, have far-reaching effects on reading skills and the use of appropriate syntactic forms. Stimulation of this area facilitates improved awareness of phonemic similarities and differences in isolation and in meaningful semantic units, which are essential for the development of reading and verbal expression skills.

Task A: Discrimination of Minimal Pairs

I'm going to say two words. You tell me if the words are the same or different.

s = same; d = different

1. pin - been (d)
2. hat - hat (s)
3. day - play (d)
4. meat - neat (d)
5. lot - lot (s)
6. share - chair (d)
7. car - bar (d)
8. ride - ride (s)
9. free - tree (d)
10. play - lay (d)
11. block - lock (d)
12. rain - train (d)
13. fox - fox (s)
14. mine - man (d)
15. win - win (s)
16. ten - tan (d)
17. ride - red (d)
18. got - goat (d)
19. pin - pin (s)
20. read - read (s)
21. clock - clack (d)
22. tent - tint (d)
23. fix - fit (d)

24. gate - gate (s)
25. not - knot (s)
26. back - bat (d)
27. beer - bean (d)
28. wet - wet (s)
29. hat - ham (d)
30. near - neat (d)
31. car - car (s)
32. sing - sink (d)
33. rope - wrote (d)
34. pan - pant (d)
35. raise - raise (s)
36. wish - witch (d)
37. weigh - weight (d)
38. day - date (d)
39. floor - floor (s)
40. rack - rack (s)
41. cow - cowl (d)
42. knob - fob (d)
43. tale - tale (s)
44. cool - cool (s)
45. beat - meat (d)
46. set - sit (d)

47. rock - sock (d)   49. knock - knock (s)

48. book - book (s)   50. glass - grass (d)

I.E.P. Goal: The client will discriminate two monosyllabic meaningful words as being the same or different when presented aloud with 90% or greater accuracy.

Auditory Discrimination
Task B: Yes/No Response for Initial Sound Discrimination in Words

We're going to think about the first sound of different words.   Listen carefully.

y = yes; n = no

1. Do these words start with the /m/ sound?   Answer yes or no.

man (y)	match (y)	cup (n)
box (n)	mix (y)	milk (y)
mom (y)	paper (n)	maybe (y)
bomb (n)	pat (n)	motorcycle (y)

2. Do these words start with the /p/ sound?

pop (y)	ox (n)	help (n)
pan (y)	pit (y)	play (y)
put (y)	push (y)	wind (n)
cup (n)	up (n)	pickle (y)

3. Do these words start with the /n/ sound?

on (n)	nest (y)	neat (y)
never (y)	pen (n)	make (n)
no (y)	win (n)	noise (y)
new (y)	nook (y)	nickel (y)

4. Do these words start with the /k/ sound?

corn (y)	stick (n)	can (y)
ketchup (y)	key (y)	car (y)
cook (y)	bacon (n)	knock (n)
truck (n)	box (n)	desk (n)

5. Do these words start with the /b/ sound?

boat (y)	crab (n)	boot (y)
tuba (n)	broom (y)	barrel (y)
sink (n)	box (y)	camera (n)
boy (y)	pig (n)	purse (n)

9

6. Do these words start with the /t/ sound?

tennis (y)	kind (n)	tire (y)
trunk (y)	tomatoes (y)	towel (y)
shoe (n)	kite (n)	clock (n)
fight (n)	ticket (y)	book (n)

7. Do these words start with the /l/ sound?

fat (n)	lily (y)	lady (y)
watch (n)	bike (n)	wheel (n)
line (y)	whale (n)	light (y)
lion (y)	log (y)	steam (n)

8. Do these words start with the /r/ sound?

rock (y)	run (y)	lead (n)
water (n)	raccoon (y)	raft (y)
ring (y)	grass (n)	rescue (y)
weeds (n)	little (n)	stool (n)

9. Do these words start with the /s/ sound?

sugar (n)	game (n)	Sally (y)
sandwich (y)	thimble (n)	smack (y)
switch (y)	boys (n)	glass (n)
sauce (y)	zipper (n)	scooter (y)

10. Do these words start with the /ā/ sound?

acorn (y)	apple (n)	auction (n)
able (y)	alligator (n)	every (n)
airplane (y)	although (n)	amen (y)
actual (n)	ale (y)	alien (y)

11. Do these words start with the /f/ sound?

fox (y)	float (y)	vow (n)
fairy (y)	forlorn (y)	tire (n)
vase (n)	knife (n)	muffin (n)
fat (y)	fire (y)	forest (y)

12. Do these words start with the /ō/ sound?

open (y)	owl (n)	ocean (y)
olive (n)	over (y)	okra (y)
oak (y)	octopus (n)	out (n)
buoy (n)	hello (n)	otter (n)

10

13. Do these words start with the /w/ sound?

window (y)	watch (y)	paw (n)
lamp (n)	watermelon (y)	worm (y)
lend (n)	bill (n)	walnut (y)
bow (n)	wall (y)	lawn (n)

14. Do these words start with the /d/ sound?

dust (y)	dirt (y)	mud (n)
ditch (y)	doughnuts (y)	board (n)
lady (n)	tree (n)	book (n)
tab (n)	bad (n)	danger (y)

15. Do these words start with the /ch/ sound?

chop (y)	chestnut (y)	char (y)
chew (y)	certainly (n)	ship (n)
shadow (n)	challenge (y)	share (n)
slippery (n)	cherry (y)	cherish (y)

16. Do these words start with the /ē/ sound?

each (y)	empty (n)	equal (y)
eat (y)	eel (y)	extra (n)
bee (n)	eye (n)	bell (n)
ear (y)	tire (n)	east (y)

17. Do these words start with the /h/ sound?

hoe (y)	hook (y)	children (n)
hatchet (y)	branch (n)	hole (y)
shutter (n)	hen (y)	wind (n)
wheel (n)	helicopter (y)	hard (y)

18. Do these words start with the /ī/ sound?

icicle (y)	sign (n)	ice cream (y)
pipe (n)	even (n)	idle (y)
inn (n)	ice (y)	cliff (n)
isle (y)	island (y)	bridge (n)

19. Do these words start with the /z/ sound?

sick (n)	slipper (n)	zealous (y)
zebra (y)	zigzag (y)	zany (y)
zipper (y)	shoulder (n)	show (n)
sandwich (n)	chair (n)	zoo (y)

20. Do these words start with the /v/ sound?

vase (y)	Vincent (y)	very (y)
van (y)	television (n)	vine (y)
violets (y)	voyage (y)	box (n)
glove (n)	berry (n)	window (n)

I.E.P. Goal: The client will answer yes or no appropriately when asked about the presence of a specific phoneme in the initial position of the word presented aloud with 90% or greater accuracy.

Auditory Discrimination
Task C: Generation of Words from Specific Initial Sounds

I'll tell you a sound. Then, you tell me a word that begins with that sound.

1. /p/	(pan, put)	14. /t/	(top, tip)
2. /m/	(man, mix)	15. /d/	(dog, dad)
3. /n/	(now, next)	16. /ō/	(open, owe)
4. /w/	(wind, watch)	17. /h/	(house, hat)
5. /k/	(keep, kitchen)	18. /z/	(zebra, zoo)
6. /g/	(gun, glass)	19. /ē/	(eat, eel)
7. /l/	(lamp, lift)	20. /ī/	(ice, icicle)
8. /s/	(sandwich, sun)	21. /j/	(jump, jeep)
9. /f/	(feet, fan)	22. /y/	(yellow, yell)
10. /sh/	(shoulder, shadow)	23. /ū/	(ukelele, unicorn)
11. /ch/	(churn, chop)	24. /v/	(vase, vow)
12. /b/	(box, bed)	25. /ā/	(able, acorn)
13. /r/	(red, rooster)		

I.E.P. Goal: The client will generate a meaningful word beginning with a specific phoneme presented aloud with 90% or greater accurcacy.

Task D: Yes/No Response for Final Sound Discrimination in Words

We're going to think about the last sound of different words. Listen carefully.

1. Do these words end with the /s/ sound? Answer yes or no.

ice (y)	nest (n)	sick (n)
may (n)	is (n)	miss (y)
zoo (n)	soup (n)	pace (y)
cup (n)	nice (y)	next (n)

2. Do these words end with the /k/ sound?

pack (y)	pig (n)	cake (y)
rake (y)	pen (n)	cave (n)
rug (n)	rock (y)	bug (n)
light (n)	sock (y)	nickel (n)

3. Do these words end with the /n/ sound?

nine (y)	bench (n)	sun (y)
bin (y)	hen (y)	skin (y)
crane (y)	balloon (y)	hand (n)
numb (n)	nose (n)	long (n)

4. Do these words end with the /g/ sound?

fog (y)	sponge (n)	iceberg (y)
bud (n)	dog (y)	need (n)
big (y)	twig (y)	bag (y)
log (y)	side (n)	kid (n)

5. Do these words end with the /b/ sound?

cab (y)	knob (y)	club (y)
job (y)	cave (n)	slob (y)
drive (n)	tub (y)	globe (y)
rib (y)	crib (y)	brave (n)

6. Do these words end with the /t/ sound?

sad (n)	light (y)	lock (n)
heat (y)	rock (n)	wait (y)
bat (y)	bake (n)	date (y)
make (n)	meat (y)	fig (n)

7. Do these words end with the /l/ sound?

pow (n)	chill (y)	gip (n)
pole (y)	wake (n)	fill (y)
shawl (y)	buff (n)	heel (y)
nail (y)	goal (y)	give (n)

8. Do these words end with the /r/ sound?

fear (y)	ear (y)	lollipop (n)
fur (y)	your (y)	river (y)
cow (n)	drip (n)	roll (n)
bird (n)	paper (y)	store (y)

9. Do these words end with the /ā/ sound?

stay (y)	hay (y)	raisin (n)
ape (n)	pail (n)	apron (n)
and (n)	they (y)	bay (y)
spray (y)	gray (y)	day (y)

10. Do these words end with the /f/ sound?

have (n)	roof (y)	hit (n)
if (y)	vase (n)	wash (n)
life (y)	chef (y)	cough (y)
door (n)	behave (n)	loaf (y)

11. Do these words end with the /ch/ sound?

chair (n)	lurch (y)	light (n)
church (y)	miss (n)	asks (n)
fish (n)	arch (y)	bench (y)
perch (y)	radish (n)	beach (y)

12. Do these words end with the /ō/ sound?

go (y)	oak (n)	grow (y)
boat (n)	acre (n)	place (n)
hoe (y)	say (n)	about (n)
toe (y)	no (y)	throw (y)

13. Do these words end with the /sh/ sound?

church (n)	rich (n)	finish (y)
wash (y)	trash (y)	peach (n)
bush (y)	bit (n)	switch (n)
speech (n)	cash (y)	crash (y)

14. Do these words end with the /d/ sound?

add (y)	coat (n)	hard (y)
sad (y)	shade (y)	ride (y)
kit (n)	lemonade (y)	keep (n)
eight (n)	kid (y)	teach (n)

15. Do these words end with the /ē/ sound?

if (n)	him (n)	teacher (n)
bee (y)	fish (n)	sheep (n)
key (y)	tree (y)	free (y)
tea (y)	thirty (y)	agree (y)

16. Do these words end with the /ī/ sound?

hour (n)	night (n)	sky (y)
eyes (n)	shy (y)	find (n)
my (y)	play (n)	dive (n)
vow (n)	cry (y)	tire (n)

17. Do these words end with the /ū/ sound?

few (y)	pew (y)	by (n)
plow (n)	view (y)	chew (y)
cue (y)	use (n)	came (n)
house (n)	boy (n)	hue (y)

18. Do these words end with the /m/ sound?

drum (y)	mom (y)	lend (n)
arm (y)	rim (y)	land (n)
smoke (n)	limb (y)	farm (y)
bump (n)	limp (n)	skim (y)

19. Do these words end with the /v/ sound?

half (n)	oak (n)	hive (y)
wave (y)	glove (y)	save (y)
stove (y)	touch (n)	move (y)
life (n)	gruff (n)	giraffe (n)

20. Do these words end with the /z/ sound?

use (n)	is (y)	cheese (y)
noise (y)	gas (n)	face (n)
hose (y)	juice (n)	big (n)
bus (n)	fizz (y)	rice (n)

I.E.P. Goal: The client will answer yes or no appropriately when asked about the presence of a specific phoneme in the final position of the word with 90% or greater accuracy.

Auditory Discrimination
Task E: Discrimination of Word Endings as being the Same or Different

I'll say two words.   You tell me if the words have the same last sound or different last sounds.   Listen carefully.

1. hot - lot (s)
2. bid - book (d)
3. sit - kit (s)
4. seem - dream (s)
5. bill - fill (s)
6. chair - crash (d)
7. ice - is (d)
8. knife - have (d)
9. bug - egg (s)
10. orange - fudge (s)
11. jail - nail (s)
12. jack - pat (d)
13. jeep - slap (s)
14. corn - bin (s)
15. arm - swan (d)
16. park - make (s)
17. pea - fee (s)
18. act - rack (d)
19. hop - Bob (d)
20. rate - sat (s)
21. door - chair (s)
22. roll - now (d)
23. shore - more (s)

24. sun - nine (s)
25. break - fate (d)
26. sing - ring (s)
27. shoot - rook (d)
28. shy - fly (s)
29. brush - witch (d)
30. face - raise (d)
31. pet - got (s)
32. theme - calm (s)
33. thief - if (s)
34. pick - pig (d)
35. mom - farm (s)
36. this - miss (s)
37. vain - train (s)
38. whip - sip (s)
39. nerve - have (s)
40. which - wish (d)
41. quail - crow (d)
42. zoo - boot (d)
43. bat - back (d)
44. wind - Maine (d)
45. twine - mine (s)
46. mug - mud (d)

47. did - trip (d)   49. slob - cave (d)

48. notch - sketch (s)   50. plant - left (s)

I.E.P. Goal: The client will discriminate two monosyllabic words presented aloud as ending the same or differently with 90% or greater accuracy.

Auditory Discrimination
Task F: Choosing Rhyming Words

Some words have endings that sound the same or almost the same. We say those words rhyme, like *cat - hat* or *bend - friend*. I'll say some words. I want you to tell me which word doesn't rhyme with the others. Listen carefully.

Three Words

1. peach - band - hand (peach)

2. put - foot - plant (plant)

3. box - fox - door (door)

4. book - car - took (car)

5. tire - lay - fire (lay)

6. fit - sing - ping (fit)

7. dream - chair - cream (chair)

8. jump - dump - shoe (shoe)

9. wall - can - fan (wall)

10. ham - fat - lamb (fat)

11. dog - fog - nose (nose)

12. mad - sack - knack (mad)

13. rake - fake - weed (weed)

14. men - rot - ten (rot)

15. field - hay - play (field)

16. pond - fond - bee (bee)

17. saw - raw - fence (fence)

18. well - nail - smell (nail)

19. nut - brick - sick (nut)

20. duck - bear - tear (duck)

21. moss - toss - horse (horse)

22. friend - pot - send (pot)

23. hide - cook - fried (cook)

24. lamp - camp - cat (cat)

25. kite - sand - land (kite)

26. smoke - yoke - right (right)

27. room - house - flume (house)

28. sink - stink - ring (ring)

29. wet - peg - keg (wet)

30. hall - fall - caught (caught)

31. pear - glass - stair (glass)

32. plate - mate - fast (fast)

33. beef - teeth - Keith (beef)

34. lid - jam - kid (jam)

35. hot - rope - hope (hot)

36. meat - tense - fence (meat)

37. paint - faint - ten (ten)

38. bold - dirt - flirt (bold)

39. file - pale - pile (pale)

40. glue - shoe - now (now)

41. plane - jet - mane (jet)

42. blimp - shrimp - keep (keep)

43. tail - light - fight (tail)

44. train - main - fire (fire)

45. pink - sank - fink (sank)

46. seed - plead - plant (plant)

47. grape - salt - fault (grape)

48. soup - group - great (great)

49. tube - scales - males (tube)

50. suit - hair - root (hair)

Four Words

1. shirt - skirt - flirt - suit (suit)

2. tie - fly - sit - rye (sit)

3. hen - pen - Ben - tan (tan)

4. keep - drop - sleep - peep (drop)

5. dry - skit - fit - hit (dry)

6. floor - poor - hot - more (hot)

7. bun - fun - run - hat (hat)

8. rock - sit - sock - mock (sit)

9. box - fox - hand - rocks (hand)

10. deer - fear - tear - far (far)

11. zoo - ox - moo - chew (ox)

12. pad - mad - pod - sad (pod)

13. mat - make - shake - fake (mat)

14. sketch - stretch - fetch - call (call)

15. smoke - smock - clock - rock (smoke)

16. green - tree - scene - lean (tree)

17. ring - king - sing - song (song)

18. ant - rant - rake - pant (rake)

19. spool - tale - fool - tool (tale)

20. bead - book - feed - seed (book)

21. met - bell - tell - sell (met)

22. sharp - harp - hook - carp (hook)

23. stove - bank - sank - rank (stove)

24. float - note - tote - take (take)

25. muss - bus - rust - pus (rust)

26. fine - match - pine - sign (match)

27. pill - par - far - car (pill)

28. balk - chalk - sick - walk (sick)

29. tooth - toast - couth - booth (toast)

30. hill - pill - fill - nail (nail)

31. fog - hog - food - log (food)

32. chill - rag - dill - mill (rag)

33. host - most - mail - ghost (mail)

34. keel - sail - nail - pail (keel)

35. paste - haste - waste - make (make)

36. hood - should - would - care (care)

18

37. hop - sleep - peep - keep (hop)

38. tow - row - sew - knew (knew)

39. dust - rust - lack - lust (lack)

40. gold - fold - hold - roll (roll)

41. fib - crib - rib - rag (rag)

42. thin - pan - tin - pin (pan)

43. char - far - star - pack (pack)

44. shoe - rage - cage - sage (shoe)

45. hose - freeze - rose - nose (freeze)

46. nest - best - hair - test (hair)

47. reach - beach - teach - learn (learn)

48. fort - port - knock - short (knock)

49. rake - fake - pot - make (pot)

50. rock - stone - phone - drone (rock)

I.E.P. Goal: The client will discriminate which word in a list of three or four monosyllabic words presented aloud does not rhyme with the others with 90% accuracy or greater.

Auditory Discrimination
Task G: Generation of Rhyming Words

I'll say a word.   Then, you tell me a word that rhymes with the word I say.

1. door (floor)

2. cat (hat)

3. wire (fire)

4. chin (pin)

5. snow (show)

6. deer (peer)

7. stair (hair)

8. reach (teach)

9. mail (sail)

10. mad (sad)

11. men (ten)

12. right (night)

13. rock (sock)

14. hand (sand)

15. pig (wig)

16. plant (chant)

17. drop (chop)

18. tan (pan)

19. put (foot)

20. fox (box)

21. keep (cheap)

22. hit (fit)

23. floor (poor)

24. wrench (bench)

25. book (hook)

26. chip (clip)

27. fly (rye)

28. dock (clock)

29. pond (fond)

30. pole (hole)

31. brook (cook)

32. cave (save)

33. scream (team)

34. sled (head)

35. pipe (ripe)

36. skis (fleas)

37. waist (paste)

38. bee (see)

39. rice (nice)

40. heel (feel)

41. dot (pot)

42. spool (cool)

43. shell (bell)

44. chest (best)

45. wall (hall)

46. goat (float)

47. ball (fall)

48. paint (faint)

49. smoke (choke)

50. toast (coast)

I.E.P. Goal: *The client will generate a rhyming word retaining the final sound when presented with a monosyllabic word aloud with 90% accuracy or greater.*

Auditory Discrimination
Task H: Yes/No Response for Medial Sound Discrimination in Words

We're going to listen for the sound in the middle of a word.   Listen carefully.

1.   Do these words have the /m/ sound in the middle?   Answer yes or no.

summer (y)	funny (n)	comedy (y)
rummy (y)	tomato (y)	panic (n)
running (n)	limit (y)	comic (y)
sleeping (n)	couple (n)	bonus (n)

2.   Do these words have the /p/ sound in the middle?

open (y)	stupid (y)	bunny (n)
puppy (y)	swig (n)	topic (y)
cowboy (n)	hotdog (n)	couple (y)
rabbit (n)	soapy (y)	league (n)

3.   Do these words have the /n/ sound in the middle?

lemon (n)	salute (n)	tennis (y)
honey (y)	finish (y)	comedy (n)
bunny (y)	banana (y)	button (n)
jelly (n)	summer (n)	dinner (y)

4. Do these words have the /k/ sound in the middle?

ticket (y)	bitter (n)	better (n)
racket (y)	rocket (y)	forget (n)
locket (y)	August (n)	chicken (y)
sailor (n)	begin (n)	bucket (y)

5. Do these words have the /g/ sound in the middle?

begin (y)	shawl (n)	cigar (y)
eager (y)	Oregon (y)	puddle (n)
behind (n)	sugar (y)	hamburger (y)
daily (n)	window (n)	forgive (y)

6. Do these words have the /b/ sound in the middle?

baby (y)	today (n)	lobby (y)
mirror (n)	ribbon (y)	robot (y)
bubbles (y)	obey (y)	urgent (n)
rabbit (y)	tiger (n)	pageant (n)

7. Do these words have the /t/ sound in the middle?

nutty (y)	daughter (y)	kitten (y)
ticket (n)	better (y)	necklace (n)
beauty (y)	pity (y)	nibble (n)
knocker (n)	canyon (n)	notice (y)

8. Do these words have the /l/ sound in the middle?

collie (y)	cellar (y)	jolly (y)
olive (y)	power (n)	pillar (y)
sour (n)	Jell-O (y)	shovel (n)
yellow (y)	velvet (y)	worry (n)

9. Do these words have the /r/ sound in the middle?

rocket (n)	sheriff (y)	sorry (y)
hero (y)	carrot (y)	allowance (n)
forest (y)	towel (n)	carol (y)
plowing (n)	giraffe (y)	whisper (n)

10. Do these words have the /s/ sound in the middle?

policeman (y)	Lucy (y)	dessert (n)
bicycle (y)	music (n)	baseball (y)
possible (y)	napkin (n)	fancy (y)
scissors (n)	razor (n)	blessing (y)

11. Do these words have the /ch/ sound in the middle?

better (n)	preacher (y)	matches (y)
teacher (y)	roaches (y)	planting (n)
patches (y)	fishing (n)	coaches (y)
washing (n)	catching (y)	picture (y)

12. Do these words have the /f/ sound in the middle?

river (n)	gopher (y)	coffeepot (y)
laughing (y)	office (y)	movie (n)
rifle (y)	sitting (n)	coffin (y)
beaver (n)	washing (n)	Goofy (y)

13. Do these words have the /ĭ/ sound in the middle?

bill (y)	wish (y)	milk (y)
these (n)	ball (n)	king (y)
fish (y)	is (n)	tea (n)
six (y)	insult (n)	every (n)

14. Do these words have the /w/ sound in the middle?

flower (y)	roller (n)	hour (y)
aware (y)	blower (y)	shower (y)
really (n)	lower (y)	sewer (y)
Virginia (n)	acorn (n)	wrestler (n)

15. Do these words have the /d/ sound in the middle?

paddle (y)	ready (y)	dungeon (n)
muddy (y)	pudding (y)	ranger (n)
label (n)	teaching (n)	window (y)
little (n)	meadow (y)	lady (y)

16. Do these words have the /ē/ sound in the middle?

feet (y)	wheel (y)	green (y)
sleep (y)	elephant (n)	bead (y)
if (n)	teacher (y)	idiot (y)
she (n)	please (y)	pack (n)

17. Do these words have the /h/ sound in the middle?

middle (n)	grasshopper (y)	tomahawk (y)
somehow (y)	treehouse (y)	reheat (y)
behold (y)	cinnamon (n)	daily (n)
careless (n)	weekly (n)	Ohio (y)

18. Do these words have the /z/ sound in the middle?

trouser (y)	amazing (y)	kettle (n)
rosy (y)	nasal (y)	razor (y)
Louisa (y)	nasty (n)	table (n)
scary (n)	lousy (y)	reliable (n)

19. Do these words have the /v/ sound in the middle?

heaven (y)	living (y)	eleven (y)
waffle (n)	river (y)	Navy (y)
neighbor (n)	fable (n)	beaver (y)
oven (y)	very (n)	rabbit (n)

20. Do these words have the /ă/ sound in the middle?

back (y)	tan (y)	ran (y)
ax (n)	dash (y)	box (n)
about (n)	dirt (n)	began (y)
had (y)	day (n)	bag (y)

I.E.P. Goal: The client will respond yes or no appropriately when asked whether a word presented aloud contains a specific phoneme in the medial position with 90% or greater accuracy.

Auditory Discrimination
Task I: Discrimination of Phonemic Similarities in Words

I'll say two words. You tell me which sound is the same in those two words. For example, if I say "hop - sleep," you would say they both have the "p" sound at the end. Let's try some.

1. arm - ram (m)	11. dirt - sat (t)
2. night - never (n)	12. fur - door (r)
3. not - but (t)	13. hat - hog (h)
4. dogs - bees (z)	14. around - carrots (r)
5. owl - ball (l)	15. cowboy - corn (c)
6. pet - bell (e)	16. shadow - hello (o)
7. etching - reaching (ch)	17. table - above (b)
8. dock - day (d)	18. ring - sing (ing)
9. bookcase - bear (b)	19. fire - fast (f)
10. pillow - Sally (l)	20. fish - bit (i)

21. ghost - gate (g)

22. clock - clack (cl)

23. cup - bus (u)

24. face - ice (s)

25. eel - equal (e)

26. Jell-0 - jar (j)

27. nail - ball (l)

28. happy - supper (p)

29. valentine - veal (v)

30. shower - away (w)

31. zoo - zebra (z)

32. year - yellow (y)

33. hardware - pudding (d)

34. knowing - night (n)

35. attend - baton (t)

36. tough - calf (f)

37. eleven - petting (e)

38. gruff - great (gr)

39. fly - flip (fl)

40. oaf - oak (o)

41. roof - razor (r)

42. witch - catch (ch)

43. forest - best (st)

44. sweater - swirl (sw)

45. oranges - dungeon (j)

46. lemon - lady (l)

47. duty - necktie (t)

48. matter - pal (a)

49. thank - thud (th)

50. quit - quiz (kw)

I.E.P. Goal: *The client will discriminate the phonemic similarity between two words presented aloud with 90% or greater accuracy.*

Auditory Discrimination
Task J: Discrimination of Phonemic Differences in Words

I'll say two words. You tell me which sound is different in those two words. For example, if I say "top - mop," you would say one starts with "t" and the other starts with "m." Let's try some.

1. bed - red (b, r)

2. car - card (d)

3. dog - dogs (z)

4. tack - stack (s)

5. how - cow (h, c)

6. leaf - leak (f, k)

7. hand - sand (h, s)

8. box - fox (b, f)

9. picture - pitcher (k, t)

10. back - sack (b, s)

11. fit - fat (i, a)

12. bossy - mossy (b, m)

13. gave - give (a, i)

14. money - honey (m, h)

15. me - my (e, i)

16. groan - phone (gr, f)

17. vest - best (v, b)

18. beg - bet (g, t)

19. hug - hag (u, a)

20. flag - flack (g, k)

21. paper - caper (p, k)

22. shoot - root (sh, r)

23. leave - weave (l, w)

24. fickle - nickel (f, n)

25. pair - hair (p, h)

26. gate - mate (g, m)

27. coal - coat (l, t)

28. night - fight (n, f)

29. wake - rake (w, r)

30. sinking - thinking (s, th)

31. jelly - Jell-O (e, o)

32. moose - goose (m, g)

33. rut - nut (r, n)

34. heat - feet (h, f)

35. nose - hose (n, h)

36. verse - terse (v, t)

37. crush - crutch (sh, ch)

38. sip - zip (s, z)

39. snow - slow (sn, sl)

40. dairy - fairy (d, f)

41. why - weigh (i, a)

42. yank - plank (y, pl)

43. shirt - flirt (sh, fl)

44. brave - save (br, s)

45. no - flow (n, fl)

46. speed - reed (sp, r)

47. drank - drink (a, i)

48. scatter - splatter (sk, spl)

49. nest - next (st, kst)

50. block - rock (bl, r)

I.E.P. Goal: The client will discriminate the phonemic difference between two words presented aloud with 90% or greater accuracy.

Auditory Discrimination
Task K: Generation of Words by Altering One Sound of a Given Word

I'll say a word. You tell me another word that is the same except for one sound. For example, if I say "map," you could say "lap" or "mat." Let's try some.

1. sand (send, band)

2. bin (ban, sin)

3. tug (rug, tag)

4. fan (ran, fin)

5. bat (fat, bit)

6. hit (hat, sit)

7. set (bet, sat)

8. end (and, bend)

9. fat (cat, fit)

10. him (his, ham)

11. cup (cap, cut)

12. dog (fog, dig)

13. tap (rap, tag)

14. pan (pin, fan)

15. lid (lip, lad)

16. box (fox, rocks)

17. hair (fair, hire)

18. stock (stack, stop)

19. jar (far, car)

20. phone (fun, tone)

21. glass (glad, gloss)

22. ring (sing, rang)

23. salt (fault, malt)

24. deck (dock, peck)

25. leaf (leap, leak)

26. foot (soot, feet)

27. top (hop, tap)

28. robe (rose, rib)

29. fire (tire, for)

30. gate (late, gape)

31. light (fight, late)

32. wig (wag, pig)

33. jump (lump, bump)

34. corn (horn, torn)

35. moose (goose, mice)

36. net (get, knit)

37. pot (hot, pit)

38. sick (tick, sack)

39. pond (fond, bond)

40. tall (ball, tell)

41. zoo (boo, moo)

42. vote (coat, moat)

43. match (catch, latch)

44. wait (wear, gait)

45. van (vine, ban)

46. lung (rung, sung)

47. math (bath, wrath)

48. yell (yes, bell)

49. sour (power, tower)

50. beak (teak, bake)

I.E.P. Goal: The client will generate a word similar to the word presented aloud by altering one sound with 90% or greater accuracy.

Task L: Identification of Presence or Absence of a Syllable in a Word

We're going to listen for words that can be parts of other words.   Listen carefully.

1. Do you hear <u>meet</u> in the word meat? (y)

    meeting? (y)
    maybe? (n)
    meteor? (y)
    metal? (n)

2. Do you hear <u>bake</u> in the word baby? (n)

    bacon? (y)
    baking? (y)
    book? (n)
    back? (n)

3. Do you hear <u>book</u> in the word handbook? (y)

    bookbag? (y)
    basketball? (n)
    bookie? (y)
    broker? (n)

4. Do you hear <u>an</u> in the word finger? (n)

    fan? (y)
    animal? (y)
    pan? (y)
    box? (n)

5. Do you hear <u>pen</u> in the word pencil? (y)

    Popsicle? (n)
    pigpen? (y)
    pickle? (n)
    pens? (y)

6. Do you hear <u>die</u> in the word dime? (y)

    dryer? (n)
    diet? (y)
    dial? (y)
    radio? (n)

7. Do you hear <u>bat</u> in the word rabbit? (n)

    battery? (y)
    apartment? (n)
    combat? (y)
    acrobat? (y)

8. Do you hear <u>key</u> in the word bakery? (n)

                         keen? (y)
                         lucky? (y)
                         keystone? (y)
                         turkey? (y)

9. Do you hear <u>ate</u> in the word late? (y)

                         parrot? (n)
                         freight? (y)
                         basement? (n)
                         rating? (y)

10. Do you hear <u>beer</u> in the word berry? (n)

                         beard? (y)
                         bar? (n)
                         board? (n)
                         bear? (n)

11. Do you hear <u>row</u> in the word tomorrow? (y)

                         rotary? (y)
                         rope? (y)
                         ear? (n)
                         road? (y)

12. Do you hear <u>phone</u> in the word telephone? (y)

                         television? (n)
                         phonograph? (y)
                         megaphone? (y)
                         valentine? (n)

13. Do you hear <u>fan</u> in the word fantasy? (y)

                         fortune? (n)
                         fantastic? (y)
                         fancy? (y)
                         butterfly? (n)

14. Do you hear <u>cup</u> in the word cupboard? (n)

                         cupcake? (y)
                         cucumber? (n)
                         couple? (y)
                         candy? (n)

15. Do you hear <u>can</u> in the word candle? (y)

                         cancer? (y)
                         candor? (y)
                         camel? (n)
                         corncob? (n)

16. Do you hear <u>tie</u> in the word table? (n)
    tiger? (y)
    typhoon? (y)
    typewriter? (y)
    tunnel? (n)

17. Do you hear <u>box</u> in the word sandbox? (y)
    boxer? (y)
    foxy? (n)
    lunchbox? (y)
    baker? (n)

18. Do you hear <u>neck</u> in the word necklace? (y)
    bottleneck? (y)
    necktie? (y)
    knock? (n)
    never? (n)

19. Do you hear <u>hand</u> in the word handsome? (y)
    handful? (y)
    hamburger? (n)
    happy? (n)
    backhand? (y)

20. Do you hear <u>aim</u> in the word ankle? (n)
    blame? (y)
    ample? (n)
    aimless? (y)
    amicable? (n)

21. Do you hear <u>rough</u> in the word ruffle? (y)
    rankle? (n)
    roughneck? (y)
    rubble? (n)
    roughly? (y)

22. Do you hear <u>arm</u> in the word army? (y)
    hire? (n)
    armada? (y)
    harm? (y)
    charm? (y)

23. Do you hear <u>pick</u> in the word picture? (y)
    pitcher? (n)
    picnic? (y)
    aspic? (y)
    pack? (n)

24. Do you hear <u>pay</u> in the word paint? (y)
                                  paper? (y)
                                  peace? (n)
                                  pace? (y)
                                  pack? (n)

25. Do you hear <u>full</u> in the word fill? (n)
                                  future? (n)
                                  fulfillment? (y)
                                  fulcrum? (y)
                                  falter? (n)

26. Do you hear <u>miss</u> in the word mistake? (y)
                                  remiss? (y)
                                  matter? (n)
                                  mister? (y)
                                  middle? (n)

27. Do you hear <u>duct</u> in the word deduction? (n)
                                  duck? (n)
                                  viaduct? (y)
                                  induce? (n)
                                  aqueduct? (y)

28. Do you hear <u>cur</u> in the word current? (y)
                                  concur? (y)
                                  cursory? (y)
                                  carry? (n)
                                  customer? (n)

29. Do you hear <u>mor</u> in the word mortgage? (y)
                                  mortician? (y)
                                  immortal? (y)
                                  make? (n)
                                  mortality? (y)

30. Do you hear <u>port</u> in the word passport? (y)
                                  portal? (y)
                                  passing? (n)
                                  transport? (y)
                                  report? (y)

31. Do you hear <u>in</u> in the word insult? (y)
                                  ban? (n)
                                  fin? (y)
                                  spinner? (y)
                                  fiend? (n)

32. Do you hear <u>with</u> in the word withdrawal? (y)
         window? (n)
         notwithstanding? (y)
         withhold? (y)
         wither? (n)

33. Do you hear <u>dis</u> in the word disturb? (y)
         indiscernible? (y)
         desperate? (n)
         discard? (y)
         distance? (y)

34. Do you hear <u>tract</u> in the word tractor? (y)
         subtract? (y)
         distraction? (n)
         trapper? (n)
         trash? (n)

35. Do you hear <u>mark</u> in the word market? (y)
         maybe? (n)
         landmark? (y)
         remarkable? (y)
         mason? (n)

36. Do you hear <u>com</u> in the word common? (y)
         pommel? (n)
         intercom? (y)
         canteen? (n)
         coming? (n)

37. Do you hear <u>end</u> in the word fender? (y)
         fable? (n)
         endless? (y)
         lend? (y)
         hand? (n)

38. Do you hear <u>bor</u> in the word bored? (y)
         harbor? (n)
         broker? (n)
         cork? (n)
         border? (y)

39. Do you hear <u>ad</u> in the word advertisement? (y)
         bad? (y)
         idiot? (n)
         addition? (y)
         paddle? (y)

40. Do you hear <u>ped</u> in the word bed? (n)

                                        pedal? (y)
                                          pistol? (n)
                                          pedestrian? (y)
                                          pedestal? (y)
                                          pod? (n)

41. Do you hear <u>wall</u> in the word warping? (n)

                                          drywall? (y)
                                          well? (n)
                                          wallpaper? (y)
                                          woman? (n)

42. Do you hear <u>cam</u> in the word camera? (y)

                                          candle? (n)
                                          camping? (y)
                                          camouflage? (y)
                                          cartoon? (n)

43. Do you hear <u>tea</u> in the word teak? (y)

                                          teacher? (y)
                                          thumbtack? (n)
                                          beauty? (y)
                                          teapot? (y)

44. Do you hear <u>pack</u> in the word paper? (n)

                                          package? (y)
                                          impacted? (y)
                                          packer? (y)
                                          peck? (n)

45. Do you hear <u>bas</u> in the word basket? (y)

                                          bachelor? (n)
                                          embarassing? (n)
                                          embassy? (n)
                                          fast? (n)

46. Do you hear <u>mer</u> in the word summer? (y)

                                          mermaid? (y)
                                          master? (n)
                                          merchant? (y)
                                          mistake? (n)

47. Do you hear <u>tel</u> in the word telephone? (y)

                                          hotel? (y)
                                          telescope? (y)
                                          yodel? (n)
                                          deliver? (n)

48. Do you hear <u>cen</u> in the word century? (y)

>spicy? (n)
>center? (y)
>incentive? (y)
>screen? (n)

49. Do you hear <u>mat</u> in the word matter? (y)

>master? (n)
>matches? (y)
>magazine? (n)
>mattress? (y)

50. Do you hear <u>be</u> in the word begin? (y)

>baby? (y)
>belt? (n)
>beak? (y)
>bake? (n)

I.E.P. Goal: The client will discriminate the presence or absence of a monosyllabic word in words presented aloud with 90% or greater accuracy.

Auditory Discrimination
Task M: Discrimination of the Number of Syllables in a Word

I'll say a word.   You tell me how many syllables there are in that word.   Listen carefully.

1. cup (1)

2. shoe (1)

3. tree (1)

4. dog (1)

5. cone (1)

6. geese (1)

7. barn (1)

8. rope (1)

9. comic (2)

10. turkey (2)

11. paddle (2)

12. handle (2)

13. leader (2)

14. butter (2)

15. cotton (2)

16. window (2)

17. yogurt (2)

18. ribbon (2)

19. mushroom (2)

20. bananas (3)

21. medicine (3)

22. paperback (3)

23. handkerchief (3)

24. astronaut (3)

25. dinosaur (3)

26. gymnastics (3)

27. parasol (3)	39. hypochondriac (5)
28. calendar (3)	40. hypercritical (5)
29. appliance (3)	41. refrigerator (5)
30. directory (4)	42. hippopotamus (5)
31. thermometer (4)	43. monochromatic (5)
32. ingredient (4)	44. simultaneously (6)
33. arithmetic (4)	45. superiority (6)
34. helicopter (4)	46. deterioration (6)
35. harmonica (4)	47. autobiography (6)
36. penicillin (4)	48. deteriorative (6)
37. vegetables (3, 4)	49. individuality (7)
38. appendectomy (5)	50. materialization (7)

I.E.P. Goal: The client will discriminate the number of syllables contained in each word presented aloud with 90% or greater accuracy.

Note: These words are ordered by syllable number to facilitate use of the material in teaching the task. However, following instruction, the order should be mixed so the answers will not be obvious.

Auditory Discrimination
Task N: Discrimination of an Incorrect Word in a Sentence

I'm going to say some sentences. One word in each sentence doesn't make sense. I want you to tell me which word doesn't make sense.

1. I *rally* don't know the answer.

2. I *witch* I could go with you.

3. What do you *fink* about that?

4. The pig is *berry* fat.

5. Give the book to *ham*.

6. Elastic can *wretch* a lot.

7. We need to cut the *steams* of these flowers.

8. Please pass the salt and *paper*.

9. Turn up the *rodeo* so I can hear that song.

10. It's wet outside; you should wear your *rainboat*.

11. A *chin* is very strong if it is made of metal.

12. Has the ice *green* man been here yet?

13. The car was out of gas, so we couldn't go *shapping*.

14. Mom was changing the blankets and *shoots* on the bed.

15. The telephone will *bing* when someone is calling.

16. The *toothbash* and toothpaste are kept in the medicine cabinet.

17. The red *tock* keeps the time for the school.

18. The *tacuum* cleaner broke during the demonstration.

19. The man used the *batter* to climb up to the roof.

20. The father cut the *glass* with a lawn mower.

21. The *ramp* pole lit the roadway for the cars.

22. Children learn their ABC's in *pool*.

23. The girl's *camel* took a picture of the sailboat.

24. The children liked to jump *hope*.

25. The *garbage* fixed my broken down car.

26. My car was dirty so I went to the *car wish*.

27. The tow *trick* pulled the van out of the ditch.

28. Really ill people go to the *housepital*.

29. We bought all of our food at the *greasery* store.

30. The firefighter came and quickly put out the *tire*.

31. The *sand* shone brightly in the sky.

32. The *tanis* game was 40-0.

33. The apples are *bed*.

34. The carpets were on the *door*.

35. We paid *rant* for the apartment.

36. The barber cut the man's *heard*.

37. The kitchen had a *sank*.

38. The church *ordan* was in need of repair.

39. The iron *dressed* the wrinkles out of the shirt.

40. The *waterfelt* flowed into the river.

41. The groom wore a *bing* on his left hand.

42. The milk on the cereal was *coal*.

43. The ceiling was approximately ten *beet* high.

44. The preacher gave a *mermon*.

45. The towel was *worn* in the washing machine.

46. People go shopping on *meekdays*.

47. The school bus picks up *chickens* to take them to school.

48. The hedgetrimmer clips the *butchers* in the yard.

49. The razor *shade* off whiskers.

50. Children are to be loved by one and *ball*.

I.E.P. Goal: The client will discriminate the incorrect word in a sentence presented aloud with 90% or greater accuracy.

Auditory Discrimination
Task O: Discrimination of an Incorrect Sentence in a Paragraph

I'm going to read some short stories (paragraphs) to you.   One sentence in each story doesn't make sense.   Listen carefully and tell me which sentence doesn't make sense.

1. Fingerpainting is lots of fun.   It feels all squishy between your fingers.   *My bicycle is red.*

2. The television set was in a fine walnut cabinet.   Although it was fifteen years old, it still looked brand new.   *The dog is ill.*

3. The picture frame was an antique.   *My cat was lost on Sunday.*   Despite its cracked glass and worn finish, it still retained its beauty.

4. The pancakes tasted so good this morning.   *My car is in the shop.*   Syrup and butter made them irresistable.

5. *Jerry's pen was out of ink.*   Plants are a nice addition to a home.   Given the proper sunlight and water, they will give their owners many years of pleasure.

6. The secretary was very efficient. She was able to answer all the phone calls, keep the books, type all the letters, as well as order all the office supplies. *I feel sick today.* The company could not do without her services for more than a day!

7. Ducks are good swimmers. They paddle with their webbed feet. *Burt goes to that school.* Ducks like to eat bread which people throw in the pond.

8. Cookies are fun to make. *Be careful not to step on the flower bed.* You need flour, butter, eggs, and sugar to make sugar cookies. Some people like to add nuts, raisins or chocolate chips to cookies.

9. Early each morning, the birds begin singing outside my window. *I lost my wallet.* It is nice to wake up to the sound of birds chirping.

10. *Cars are not allowed on the sidewalks.* Swimming pools are marked for safety reasons. The deep end is roped off so that people may practice diving. The shallow end is for small children to practice swimming.

11. A good book for children to read is *Little House on the Prairie.* A television show was made from this story and is very popular. Life on the prairie wasn't always easy. The children had to work hard and help the family, but they were happy. *The movie Jaws was very scary.*

12. One summer, the Thompson family went on vacation to Colorado. Being from New York City, they had never seen wild animals outside of the zoo. They enjoyed climbing in the mountains and their walks in the woods. *The toothpaste tube was empty.* They missed their western experience when the vacation was over.

13. Every Saturday at 12 o'clock, my dad takes our new car to the carwash. We are allowed to go with him and help. My job is to dry the bumpers with a soft, dry cloth. *My brother lost his sneakers at school yesterday.* My sister is too little to help us wash the car, so she stays home with our mom.

14. When I am on a swing, I feel as if I am a bird in flight. I can go higher than the fence and the house, and sometimes I go above the trees. *Jump rope is not one of my favorite games.* But if I swing too high, the swing set comes out of the ground and I must slow down my ride.

15. *My grandmother lives in Ohio.* Last summer, I went away to camp for the first time. I rode on a bus with some other children from my town. When we arrived at camp, the counselors met us and showed us our cabin. Although it wasn't fancy, my cabin soon came to be my "home away from home."

16. Ed's father said he could get a dog for his birthday. He took him to the pet shop, but all the dogs were very expensive. *I hit a home run my third time at bat.* Then they went to the pound and Ed spied a black and white puppy. Although it was just a mutt, Ed knew that puppy was very special and took him home.

17. The circus is a fun place to spend the day. Happy and sad clowns with funny suits and painted faces walk around giving children balloons, prizes and toys. In the big circus tent, there are shows featuring trapeze artists and acrobats. *The school bus*

picks me up at eight.   The elephants at the circus give children rides on their heads and pick them up with their trunks.

18.   On a hot summer evening, we like to sit on the front porch and swing.   *The zebra has black and white stripes.*   A tall glass of homemade lemonade and gingersnap cookies somehow make the evening cooler and more enjoyable.   When the sun goes down, we turn on the outside lanterns and play a game of croquet with all the neighbors. Even though it is hot, summer is my favorite time of year.

19.   Last spring, our class took a trip to the farm. We went through the barn, the chicken coop, the farm house, and even into the pigsty. *Peanut butter cookies are made from flour, sugar, peanut butter, and butter.* Next, we watched the farmer plow a field and milk a cow. We all hoped we would own a farm one day.

20.   *Mailboxes are red, white and blue.*   Umbrellas have been around for years.   In the past, umbrellas were used a great deal to protect women's faces and shoulders from extreme sun.   Even today, large umbrellas are used on the beaches to prevent over-exposure to the sun.   Umbrellas are also still used to keep dry during wet weather.

I.E.P. Goal: The client will discriminate the incorrect sentence in a paragraph presented aloud with 90% or greater accuracy.

Auditory Discrimination: General Activities

1. Play two noisemakers in view of the student.   Then, place the noisemakers behind the student's back and play one of them.   Show them both to the student and have him choose which one was played out of his sight.

2. Use a drum, tambourine, or have the student clap his hands as you say words of varying numbers of syllables.   Ask the student to strike or clap as each syllable is pronounced and then to state the number of syllables heard.

3. Provide each student with a hand or finger counter.   This activity may be implemented in teams.   Present a sentence aloud with each student recording the syllable count contained in the sentence on their counters.   Each student is to guess how many syllables were in the sentence as recorded on their counters.   The student or students with the correct number are given 5 points.   If only one syllable off, 3 points are given and if only two syllables off, one point.   At the end of the time period, the student with the most points wins.

4. Ask the student to perform activities dependent on discrimination of the initial or final sound of a word presented as being the same or different from the first or last letter of his name.   For example, "If your name begins like 'baby', touch your head." or "If your name ends like 'candy', stand up."

5. Present a word on paper.   Ask the student to generate rhyming words by changing the first letter(s).

<u>bit</u>	<u>toy</u>
sit	boy
fit	Roy
hit	coy

6. Present a word on paper.   Ask the student to generate new words by changing the last letter(s) or medial vowel(s).
    <u>bat</u> (ba<u>g</u>, ba<u>y</u>, ba<u>d</u>, b<u>e</u>d, be<u>ll</u>, b<u>a</u>ll, bat, ba<u>d</u>, b<u>i</u>d, b<u>i</u>g)

7. When presented a nonsense syllable, the student is to generate a word that has that syllable contained in it.   For example, <u>won</u> - <u>won</u>derful, <u>won</u>der, every<u>on</u>e; <u>for</u> - <u>for</u>ward, be<u>for</u>e, un<u>for</u>tunately.

8. Tape record common environmental, animal, and musical sounds in pairs.   Some should be the same sounds (car - car) and some should be different (cat - train).   Play each sound pair for the student, who must then identify the two sounds as being the same or different.

9. Place two cards on the table depicting two objects, activities, etc., the names of which are phonemically similar (minimal pair).   Sit behind the student and name one of the pictured items.   The student responds by either picking up the card picturing the item named or repeats the name to the instructor.

39

10. Present a word to the student (noun, verb, adjective, adverb, etc.) and have the student ring a bell or raise his hand each time he hears the word in sentences presented aloud by the instructor.

Question Comprehension

Language comprehension requires processing and understanding verbal information provided through the auditory and/or visual channels. An individual's comprehension of language concepts and his ability to gain meaning from verbal material is essential as a predecessor to the use of these concepts in oral or written expression. In stimulating the area of question comprehension, a response pattern is given. This format may include a *yes/no, true/false, some/all* or an *always/sometimes/never* response. Language expansion, therefore, may occur without being impeded by deficits in verbal expression. Only with a firm basis in receptive language skills can verbal expression in meaningful units evolve.

Task A: *Can*-Questions

Circle yes or no to answer each question. The first one is done for you.

1. Can you roll a book?   yes   (no)

2. Can you stick paper together without using paste?   yes   no

3. Can you touch your ear with your nose?   yes   no

4. Can you stir something if you have a spoon?   yes   no

5. Can you brush your teeth with a comb?   yes   no

6. Can you wear your bathing suit to church?   yes   no

7. Can you step over a log?   yes   no

8. Can you eat soup with a fork?   yes   no

9. Can a couch get the measles?   yes   no

10. Can you fry eggs in a skillet?   yes   no

11. Can you drive a car with your eyes closed?   yes   no

12. Can you keep a pet elephant in your house?   yes   no

13. Can you sleep during the day?   yes   no

14. Can you look outside in the dark?   yes   no

15. Can you buy bread by the loaf?   yes   no

16. Can you teach a dog to play jacks?   yes   no

17. Can you see underwater in a swimming pool?   yes   no

18. Can bears walk on two feet?   yes   no

19. Can a lion be tamed?   yes   no

20. Can you grow a mustache on your arm?   yes   no

21. Can you drink a milk shake without using your hands? yes   no

22. Can you shovel snow with a rake?   yes   no

23. Can you stretch a brick?   yes   no

24. Can you reach your shoulder with your hand?   yes   no

25.	Can you pedal a bicycle without using your feet?	yes	no
26.	Can you blow up a balloon if it has a hole in it?	yes	no
27.	Can men have babies?	yes	no
28.	Can it rain if the sun is shining?	yes	no
29.	Can you go outside if it is raining?	yes	no
30.	Can you play the piano if you are wearing mittens?	yes	no
31.	Can you stop a runaway car by yelling at it?	yes	no
32.	Can you sing without opening your mouth?	yes	no
33.	Can a triangle have four corners?	yes	no
34.	Can gravy be frozen?	yes	no
35.	Can an octopus live out of the water?	yes	no
36.	Can you tie a paper clip?	yes	no
37.	Can you go for a ride without a car?	yes	no
38.	Can you buy meat by the pound?	yes	no
39.	Can a burned out light bulb be replaced?	yes	no
40.	Can snow tires be used during the summer?	yes	no
41.	Can you pet a porcupine easily?	yes	no
42.	Can a tall man reach higher than a short man?	yes	no
43.	Can you back up a car without putting it in reverse?	yes	no
44.	Can you breathe if you hold your nose?	yes	no
45.	Can you cut your fingernails with one hand held behind your back?	yes	no
46.	Can you make French toast without using eggs?	yes	no
47.	Can you make a jack-o'lantern from an acorn?	yes	no
48.	Can you mail a package at the post office on Sunday?	yes	no
49.	Can you ride a sheep?	yes	no

50.	Can you play tennis without a ball?	yes	no
51.	Can birds pick up objects with their wings?	yes	no
52.	Can you drink a glass of water without picking it up?	yes	no
53.	Can you climb a tree with your hands tied behind you?	yes	no
54.	Can you saw wood with a knife?	yes	no
55.	Can you stay afloat on a raft?	yes	no
56.	Can you play badminton alone?	yes	no
57.	Can you add without using a pencil?	yes	no
58.	Can you draw a straight line without using a ruler?	yes	no
59.	Can a vacuum cleaner be used on very wet carpet?	yes	no
60.	Can you board an airplane without a ticket?	yes	no
61.	Can you be arrested for obeying the law?	yes	no
62.	Can raisins be peeled?	yes	no
63.	Can penguins bend their knees?	yes	no
64.	Can gold be mined?	yes	no
65.	Can clover have four leaves?	yes	no
66.	Can you see the back of your head if you only have one mirror?	yes	no
67.	Can you make change for a quarter if you have no nickels?	yes	no
68.	Can you open an unlocked door without a key?	yes	no
69.	Can you open a bank account if you have no money?	yes	no
70.	Can distance be measured in meters?	yes	no
71.	Can a foreigner purchase land in the United States?	yes	no
72.	Can a twenty-five year old woman be elected President of the United States?	yes	no
73.	Can you vote in a national election if you are not a U.S. citizen?	yes	no

74.	Can four be divided by zero?	yes	no
75.	Can a computer be programmed?	yes	no
76.	Can you skip by using only one foot?	yes	no
77.	Can a veterinarian prescribe medicine?	yes	no
78.	Can a tourniquet stop bleeding?	yes	no
79.	Can potatoes be pared?	yes	no
80.	Can a molecule be split?	yes	no

I.E.P. Goal: *The client will answer Can-Questions correctly with 90% or greater accuracy.*

Question Comprehension
Task B: *Do/Does*-Questions

Circle yes or no to answer each question.   The first one is done for you.

1.	Does a new pair of shoes get dirty?	(yes)	no
2.	Do babies grow up to be young?	yes	no
3.	Do you get wet when you take a bath?	yes	no
4.	Does the sun make you feel warm?	yes	no
5.	Do you chew lemonade?	yes	no
6.	Does a cow wear pajamas when it sleeps?	yes	no
7.	Does a goat wear glasses?	yes	no
8.	Do pigs climb trees?	yes	no
9.	Do you put something in the trash if you want to save it?	yes	no
10.	Do roller skates have buttons?	yes	no
11.	Do golfers use clubs?	yes	no
12.	Do trained seals perform tricks?	yes	no
13.	Does a movie theater have umpires?	yes	no
14.	Does a baby bird get milk from its mother?	yes	no
15.	Does a banana have more juice than a grape?	yes	no

16.	Does a paper bag hold water?	yes	no
17.	Does an elbow bend in both directions?	yes	no
18.	Do trailers have basements?	yes	no
19.	Do caterpillars run swiftly?	yes	no
20.	Do termites eat wood?	yes	no
21.	Does a firefighter extinguish fires?	yes	no
22.	Does a broken rubber band stretch?	yes	no
23.	Does a broken refrigerator cool?	yes	no
24.	Do airplane pilots use road maps to navigate?	yes	no
25.	Does an airplane have to leave the ground before it can land?	yes	no
26.	Does a doctor listen to your heart with a stethoscope?	yes	no
27.	Does it rain in May?	yes	no
28.	Does the word *they* mean more than one person?	yes	no
29.	Do we need our hands to play a piano?	yes	no
30.	Does a doctor set a broken arm with a thermometer?	yes	no
31.	Does an airplane orbit the earth?	yes	no
32.	Do we put dirty clothes in a hamper?	yes	no
33.	Do windows have screens?	yes	no
34.	Does men's hair grow faster than women's hair?	yes	no
35.	Does an eraser get rid of a mistake?	yes	no
36.	Does a forest ranger care for wildlife?	yes	no
37.	Do you use your fingers more than your toes?	yes	no
38.	Do kites have tails?	yes	no
39.	Does Monday come before Wednesday?	yes	no
40.	Do eggs have to be broken before they are cooked?	yes	no

41. Does milk sour if it isn't refrigerated?	yes	no
42. Do automobiles have speedometers?	yes	no
43. Does a dull razor blade shave smoothly?	yes	no
44. Do neckties have pockets?	yes	no
45. Do pears contain seeds?	yes	no
46. Do electric clocks need to be wound?	yes	no
47. Does your next door neighbor live in the same city as you?	yes	no
48. Does a siren alert us to danger?	yes	no
49. Do bridges connect river banks?	yes	no
50. Does a television set get hot when you turn it on?	yes	no
51. Does a telephone directory define words?	yes	no
52. Does a camera have a lens to amplify sound?	yes	no
53. Does a microscope make large things appear smaller?	yes	no
54. Do calculators make tabulations?	yes	no
55. Does a tornado destroy property?	yes	no
56. Does an airplane take off from a station?	yes	no
57. Does your birthday always fall on the same day of the week?	yes	no
58. Does a newspaper contain a crossword puzzle?	yes	no
59. Do blacksmiths work with cloth?	yes	no
60. Does clay absorb water?	yes	no
61. Do eels live in the sea?	yes	no
62. Do matadors fight bulls?	yes	no
63. Do athletes compete in the Olympics?	yes	no
64. Do we exterminate to control insects?	yes	no
65. Do we harvest before we plant?	yes	no

66. Do soldiers perform drills?	yes	no
67. Do seat belts restrain passengers?	yes	no
68. Does a windmill produce power?	yes	no
69. Does a horse have horseshoes to protect its feet?	yes	no
70. Do the hands on a clock move in a clockwise direction?	yes	no
71. Does an engine have movable parts?	yes	no
72. Does a foreign person speak with an accent?	yes	no
73. Does a flower have roots to protect it from the wind?	yes	no
74. Does an amber light mean to slow down?	yes	no
75. Does a chemist work in a laboratory?	yes	no
76. Do televisions broadcast entertainment?	yes	no
77. Does an opera involve singers?	yes	no
78. Does a canopy lie under our feet?	yes	no
79. Does insulation protect us from extreme temperatures?	yes	no
80. Do poems convey emotions?	yes	no

I.E.P. Goal: The client will answer Do/Does-Questions correctly with 90% or greater accuracy.

Question Comprehension
Task C: *If*-Questions

Circle yes or no to answer each question.   The first one is done for you.

1. If you were a bee, could you sting?	(yes)	no
2. If you were a horse, would you have three legs?	yes	no
3. If you were a shark, could you swim under water?	yes	no
4. If you were a kangaroo, could you hop?	yes	no
5. If you were a watch, could you be wound?	yes	no
6. If you broke an egg, could you put it back together?	yes	no
7. If you have a car with a flat tire, should you drive it?	yes	no

8. If you wanted to watch a movie, would you go to a grocery store?   yes   no

9. If you were a pilot, could you fly an airplane?   yes   no

10. If something is loud, is it noisy?   yes   no

11. If you were a telephone, could you ring?   yes   no

12. If a baby cries, is it happy?   yes   no

13. If you were a parent, would you have a child?   yes   no

14. If you waited at a bus stop, could you catch a train?   yes   no

15. If it is snowing outside, is it winter?   yes   no

16. If you rip your shirt, should you glue it back together?   yes   no

17. If you need some flour, should you go to a gas station?   yes   no

18. If it is October, is Halloween near?   yes   no

19. If it is July, is it hot in Texas?   yes   no

20. If you have a necklace, do you have any jewelry?   yes   no

21. If you were a rose, would you have thorns?   yes   no

22. If you went to a rodeo, would you see a bronco?   yes   no

23. If you were a donkey, would you have fins?   yes   no

24. If you have a pencil but no paper, can you write your name?   yes   no

25. If you have a pan but no lid, can you boil water?   yes   no

26. If you are not dead, are you alive?   yes   no

27. If you get a hole in the bottom of your shoe, must you throw it away?   yes   no

28. If you're not on time, are you late?   yes   no

29. If you have a needle but no thread, can you sew?   yes   no

30. If something is heavy, can you lift it with one hand?   yes   no

31. If you were an ant, could you hide in a bottle cap?   yes   no

49

32. If you were a mouse, could you read the newspaper?   yes   no

33. If it is Wednesday, is it the weekend?   yes   no

34. If something rolls, is it round?   yes   no

35. If something is fresh, is it old?   yes   no

36. If you were a seamstress, could you make a coat?   yes   no

37. If you are broke, do you have any money?   yes   no

38. If you are a twin, are you an only child?   yes   no

39. If you had a flashlight but no batteries, could you use it?   yes   no

40. If you want to buy some nails, should you go to a hardware store?   yes   no

41. If you do not know how to swim, should you dive in the water?   yes   no

42. If you were a magician, could you perform tricks?   yes   no

43. If you had a tea bag, could you make a cup of coffee?   yes   no

44. If you had water skis but no boat, could you go skiing?   yes   no

45. If a chair is rickety, should you stand on it?   yes   no

46. If a girl wears braces, can she open her mouth?   yes   no

47. If something is frozen, is it hard?   yes   no

48. If you were a weed, could you skip?   yes   no

49. If you were a desk, could you leap?   yes   no

50. If you are an adult, are you a teenager?   yes   no

51. If you went from upstairs to the basement, would it be cooler?   yes   no

52. If you wanted to get cooled off, would you get a jacket?   yes   no

53. If you were a musician, could you play an instrument?   yes   no

54. If you have a match but no fuel, can you build a fire?   yes   no

55. If you had a scale but no yardstick, could you weigh yourself?   yes   no

56. If you play a flute, could you be a member of an orchestra?   yes   no

57. If you are rich, are you wealthy?   yes   no

58. If you are exhausted, are you tired?   yes   no

59. If you are thrifty, do you save money?   yes   no

60. If you are celebrating, are you having a good time?   yes   no

61. If two things are equal, are they identical?   yes   no

62. If something bounces, is it breakable?   yes   no

63. If something is fragile, is it strong?   yes   no

64. If something is shredded, is it whole?   yes   no

65. If something is faded, is it bright?   yes   no

66. If a woman is graceful, is she coordinated?   yes   no

67. If something is liquid, can it melt?   yes   no

68. If something splits, is it divided?   yes   no

69. If something is an antique, is it old?   yes   no

70. If something is sorrowful, is it pleasant?   yes   no

71. If you sing the national anthem, should you stand up?   yes   no

72. If a person is a preacher, is he religious?   yes   no

73. If you were traveling from Florida to Spain, could you go by train?   yes   no

74. If you pleaded guilty to a crime, would you be convicted?   yes   no

75. If something is incorrect, is it an error?   yes   no

76. If something is empty, is it void?   yes   no

77. If something is bland, is it spicy?   yes   no

78. If you were a rabbit, would you live in a burrow?   yes   no

79. If an animal is aquatic, can it swim?   yes   no

80. If you live in China, do you live in Asia?   yes   no

I.E.P. Goal: The client will answer If-Questions correctly with 90% or greater accuracy.

Question Comprehension
Task D: Quantity/Comparison Questions

Circle yes or no to answer each question.   The first one is done for you.

1.   Does a chair cost more than a map?   (yes)   no

2.   Are parents older than their children?   yes   no

3.   Does a baby weigh more than an adult?   yes   no

4.   Is your waist bigger than your neck?   yes   no

5.   Is ten less than twenty?   yes   no

6.   Is a baby younger than its mother?   yes   no

7.   Is half a banana more than two bananas?   yes   no

8.   Is a pair of socks more than one sock?   yes   no

9.   Is a pair of shoes more than three shoes?   yes   no

10.   Is a week longer than a month?   yes   no

11.   Are there ten hours in a day?   yes   no

12.   Is a hundred dollars more than fifty dollars?   yes   no

13.   Are there thirty minutes in a half-hour?   yes   no

14.   Are there more than sixty seconds in a minute?   yes   no

15.   Is a mile shorter than a yard?   yes   no

16.   Does an apple have more juice than an orange?   yes   no

17.   Does a car weigh more than a bus?   yes   no

18.   Is a size ten bigger than a size eight?   yes   no

19.   Does a large drink contain more than a medium-sized
      drink?   yes   no

20.   Is a half less than a whole?   yes   no

21.   Is one thousand a large number?   yes   no

22.   Is a foot longer than a yard?   yes   no

23. Does a week have more than five days?   yes   no

24. Is a nickel worth more than a quarter?   yes   no

25. Is a washcloth bigger than a coaster?   yes   no

26. Are ten dimes equal to a dollar?   yes   no

27. Is your ankle bigger than your knee?   yes   no

28. Is a dozen eggs more than ten eggs?   yes   no

29. Is the second person in line ahead of the fourth person?   yes   no

30. Are there ever more than 365 days in a year?   yes   no

31. Does a pound of rocks weigh more than a pound of leaves?   yes   no

32. Is a gallon of milk more than a cup?   yes   no

33. Is nine-thirty the same as half-past nine?   yes   no

34. Can a motorcycle go faster than a bicycle?   yes   no

35. Can a sailboat go faster than a yacht?   yes   no

36. Is $11.98 more than $11.95?   yes   no

37. Is one-fourth more than one?   yes   no

38. Is fifty percent the same as one half?   yes   no

39. Is a mile going uphill longer than a mile going downhill?   yes   no

40. Do any months have more than thirty days?   yes   no

41. Is a tablespoon less than a teaspoon?   yes   no

42. Is a pound more than an ounce?   yes   no

43. Does an ounce of gold weigh more than an ounce of silver?   yes   no

44. Does a quartet consist of two people?   yes   no

45. Is New York City bigger than Kansas City?   yes   no

46. Is California bigger than Rhode Island?   yes   no

47. Is a bushel more than a quart?   yes   no

48. Are eleven dimes and one quarter more than one dollar?   yes   no

49. Is an acre bigger than a square yard?   yes   no

50. Is a liter more than a cup?   yes   no

I.E.P. Goal: The client will answer Yes/No-Questions involving quantity or comparison with 90% or greater accuracy.

Question Comprehension
Task E: Noun/Verb Questions Requiring a *Yes/No* Response

Circle yes or no to answer each question. The first one is done for you.

1.	Do watches tick?	(yes)	no	20.	Do cowboys rope?	yes	no
2.	Do shoes melt?	yes	no	21.	Do ships sail?	yes	no
3.	Do girls comb?	yes	no	22.	Do carpenters build?	yes	no
4.	Do bells ring?	yes	no	23.	Do boxers fight?	yes	no
5.	Do squirrels sing?	yes	no	24.	Do ladybugs crawl?	yes	no
6.	Do flowers race?	yes	no	25.	Do shoes stretch?	yes	no
7.	Do desks jump?	yes	no	26.	Do relatives visit?	yes	no
8.	Do breezes blow?	yes	no	27.	Do numbers whistle?	yes	no
9.	Do balls bounce?	yes	no	28.	Do bricks sink?	yes	no
10.	Do sleds rip?	yes	no	29.	Do doorknobs turn?	yes	no
11.	Do daisies type?	yes	no	30.	Do bathtubs drain?	yes	no
12.	Do carrots blink?	yes	no	31.	Do ghosts haunt?	yes	no
13.	Do scissors snip?	yes	no	32.	Do maids clean?	yes	no
14.	Do cameras joke?	yes	no	33.	Does wood rot?	yes	no
15.	Do women run?	yes	no	34.	Do spoons bleed?	yes	no
16.	Do children learn?	yes	no	35.	Do shadows talk?	yes	no
17.	Do cats leap?	yes	no	36.	Do jockeys ride?	yes	no
18.	Do gloves marry?	yes	no	37.	Do knees bend?	yes	no
19.	Do police officers watch?	yes	no	38.	Do dishtowels remember?	yes	no

39.	Do waves break?	yes	no	65.	Do baskets cook?	yes	no
40.	Do shells cough?	yes	no	66.	Do elevators shrink?	yes	no
41.	Do boxes rip?	yes	no	67.	Do nurses assist?	yes	no
42.	Does hair grow?	yes	no	68.	Do principals listen?	yes	no
43.	Do pants shrink?	yes	no	69.	Do cars trip?	yes	no
44.	Do horses ride?	yes	no	70.	Do men age?	yes	no
45.	Does plastic bend?	yes	no	71.	Do gophers paint?	yes	no
46.	Do pickles melt?	yes	no	72.	Do banks salute?	yes	no
47.	Do bees pollinate?	yes	no	73.	Do boys complain?	yes	no
48.	Do weeds walk?	yes	no	74.	Do sponges absorb?	yes	no
49.	Do clams swim?	yes	no	75.	Do audiences applaud?	yes	no
50.	Do holidays sigh?	yes	no	76.	Does a match ignite?	yes	no
51.	Do actors perform?	yes	no	77.	Do people comment?	yes	no
52.	Does water flow?	yes	no	78.	Does lipstick heal?	yes	no
53.	Do butterflies waltz?	yes	no	79.	Do customers purchase?	yes	no
54.	Do blenders heat?	yes	no	80.	Do automobiles collide?	yes	no
55.	Do shorts scrub?	yes	no	81.	Do workers strike?	yes	no
56.	Do toothbrushes drill?	yes	no	82.	Do cartoons amuse?	yes	no
57.	Do vitamins hope?	yes	no	83.	Do checks bounce?	yes	no
58.	Do speakers amplify?	yes	no	84.	Do hats protect?	yes	no
59.	Do candles borrow?	yes	no	85.	Do magazines inform?	yes	no
60.	Do ropes burn?	yes	no	86.	Do balloons expand?	yes	no
61.	Do canoes sink?	yes	no	87.	Do detectives investigate?	yes	no
62.	Do pillows mourn?	yes	no	88.	Does boiling water sterilize?	yes	no
63.	Does paper crease?	yes	no	89.	Does sand attach?	yes	no
64.	Do parachutes float?	yes	no				

90. Does a bulldozer raze?	yes no	96. Do carpets navigate?	yes no
91. Do politicians campaign?	yes no	97. Do babies communicate?	yes no
92. Do swords pierce?	yes no	98. Do savings accumulate?	yes no
93. Do accountants add?	yes no	99. Do parents instruct?	yes no
94. Do students compose?	yes no	100. Do leases expire?	yes no
95. Do engineers design?	yes no		

I.E.P. Goal: *The client will answer Do/Does-Questions with a noun-verb format with 90% or greater accuracy.*

Question Comprehension
Task F: Two-Variable Questions Requiring a *Yes/No* Response

Circle yes or no to answer each question. The first one is done for you.

1. Are squirrels and rabbits small animals?   (yes)   no

2. Is ham a sour-tasting meat?   yes   no

3. Are bananas yellow fruit?   yes   no

4. Are lions and elephants good animals to have for pets?   yes   no

5. Are hoes and rakes helpful farming tools?   yes   no

6. Are Christmas trees tall flowers?   yes   no

7. Are apples and strawberries sweet-tasting vegetables?   yes   no

8. Do clocks and sundials tell you the time?   yes   no

9. Are cakes and pies sour-tasting desserts?   yes   no

10. Are candy canes red and white striped candies?   yes   no

11. Are curtains attractive shades from the afternoon sun?   yes   no

12. Are pencils and pens good writing tools for a chalkboard?   yes   no

13. Are cars and boats good means for land transportation?   yes   no

14. Can trees grow up to be underground plants?   yes   no

15. Are thermometers and stethoscopes tools for a doctor?   yes   no

16. Are rhinoceroses and gorillas tame animals?   yes   no

17. Are Alaska and Chicago both northern states?	yes	no
18. Are oaks and petunias fruit-bearing trees?	yes	no
19. Are cotton and silk smooth types of cloth?	yes	no
20. Can you watch movies on radios and cassette recorders?	yes	no
21. Are salmon and finches both types of fresh-water fish?	yes	no
22. Do raincoats and parkas protect you from the dry heat?	yes	no
23. Are trumpets and saxophones wind instruments?	yes	no
24. Do colanders and strainers help drain excess water from your food?	yes	no
25. Are dancing and farming both indoor occupations?	yes	no
26. Are the letters "l" and "m" consecutive?	yes	no
27. Are oysters and clams salt-water shellfish?	yes	no
28. Are Band-Aids and tape adhesive strips?	yes	no
29. Are mosquitos and storks large insects?	yes	no
30. Do trawlers and tankers carry cargo across the land?	yes	no
31. Are penicillin and epoxy both medicine?	yes	no
32. Can movies and paintings be appreciated visually?	yes	no
33. Are paint and syrup thick, clear liquids?	yes	no
34. Are lungs and kidneys vital body organs?	yes	no
35. Are tarantulas and copperheads dangerous insects?	yes	no

I.E.P. Goal: The client will answer questions with two variables with 90% or greater accuracy.

Question Comprehension
Task G: Mixed *Yes/No* Questions

Circle yes or no to answer each question. The first one is done for you.

1. Do all boys have freckles?	yes	(no)
2. Can you put on your pants before you put on your shirt?	yes	no
3. Can your aunt be a man?	yes	no

4. Is fifteen more than eight?   yes   no

5. If you fall into the ocean, will you get wet?   yes   no

6. Is your cousin also your sister?   yes   no

7. Could a horse weigh more than a man?   yes   no

8. Is a son older than his father?   yes   no

9. Does a refrigerator heat all of the time?   yes   no

10. Do skunks stink?   yes   no

11. Do flags flutter in the breeze?   yes   no

12. Can you read a book in the dark?   yes   no

13. If you were a tree, would you grow?   yes   no

14. If you were a fish, could you walk?   yes   no

15. If you were a bed, could you sleep?   yes   no

16. Does a knee bend?   yes   no

17. Does a book read?   yes   no

18. If you were a typewriter, could you type?   yes   no

19. If you were a road, could you travel?   yes   no

20. Is a second longer than an hour?   yes   no

21. Is an ounce more than a pound?   yes   no

22. Do people become distracted?   yes   no

23. Does the sun illuminate?   yes   no

24. If you were an athlete, would you exercise?   yes   no

25. Can copy machines duplicate?   yes   no

26. Does the earth rotate?   yes   no

27. Do radios have picture tubes?   yes   no

28. Do televisions and radios give you up-to-date news?   yes   no

29. Are hazel and brown two shades of eye color?   yes   no

30. Are hyacinths a type of flower?   yes   no

I.E.P. Goal: The client will answer a variety of questions correctly with 90% or greater accuracy.

Question Comprehension
Task H: *Some/All* Questions

Circle some or all to answer each question.   The first one is done for you.

1. Do some / all people have eyes?   some   (all)

2. Are some / all apples fruit?   some   all

3. Are some / all bottles made of glass?   some   all

4. Are some / all birthdays in June?   some   all

5. Do some / all children have brothers and sisters?   some   all

6. Do some / all fish live in the water?   some   all

7. Do some / all people have auburn hair?   some   all

8. Do some / all houses have walls?   some   all

9. Are some / all buses yellow?   some   all

10. Do some / all shirts have pockets?   some   all

11. Do some / all sweaters have V-necks?   some   all

12. Are some / all fences wooden?   some   all

13. Are some / all houses two-story?   some   all

14. Do some / all rooms have doorways?   some   all

15. Do some / all candles have wicks?   some   all

16. Do some / all books have pages?   some   all

17. Do some / all bees sting?   some   all

18. Are some / all men old?   some   all

19. Are some / all windows broken?   some   all

20. Are some / all couches soft?   some   all

21. Are some / all flowers yellow?   some   all

22. Is some / all rain wet?   some   all

23. Are some / all boys taller than girls?   some   all

24. Do some / all children go to nursery school?   some   all

25. Are some / all pencils sharp?   some   all

26. Do some / all cars use oil?   some   all

27. Do some / all teeth have cavities?   some   all

28. Are some / all dogs animals?   some   all

29. Are some / all shoes worn on the feet?   some   all

30. Are some / all people happy?   some   all

31. Are some / all singers women?   some   all

32. Do some / all jeans have legs?   some   all

33. Do some / all suits have vests?   some   all

34. Do some / all weddings have brides?   some   all

35. Do some / all trains run on tracks?   some   all

36. Are some / all days hot?   some   all

37. Are some / all trees alive?   some   all

38. Are some / all clothes too big for you?   some   all

39. Are some / all tires round?   some   all

40. Do some / all ships move in water?   some   all

41. Are some / all books good?   some   all

42. Do some / all people work?   some   all

43. Is some / all water cold?   some   all

44. Is some / all snow cold?   some   all

45. Are some / all rings size five?   some   all

46. Are some / all birds robins?   some   all

47. Are some / all men six feet tall?	some	all
48. Can some / all teenagers drive?	some	all
49. Can you see some / all the stars at night?	some	all
50. Do some / all boys like to play baseball?	some	all
51. Do some / all women wear skirts?	some	all
52. Do some / all chickens have beaks?	some	all
53. Are some / all people under ten years of age?	some	all
54. Do some / all neighbors like to fish?	some	all
55. Do some / all dogs have paws?	some	all
56. Do some / all horses have hooves?	some	all
57. Do some / all people have birthdays?	some	all
58. Is some / all tape sticky?	some	all
59. Are some / all leaves green?	some	all
60. Do some / all toes have toenails?	some	all
61. Do some / all people have a mother?	some	all
62. Do some / all men have wives?	some	all
63. Are some / all babies young?	some	all
64. Do some / all thieves steal?	some	all
65. Are some / all flags red, white and blue?	some	all
66. Are some / all elephants heavy?	some	all
67. Can some / all people sing well?	some	all
68. Do some / all days have mornings?	some	all
69. Do some / all pens use ink?	some	all
70. Are some / all children shy?	some	all
71. Do some / all fingers have knuckles?	some	all
72. Do some / all people have hearts?	some	all

73. Are some / all horses geldings?   some   all

74. Is some / all of Arizona in the United States?   some   all

75. Do some / all rectangles have four sides?   some   all

76. Are some / all days twenty-four hours long?   some   all

77. Is some / all water liquid?   some   all

78. Do some / all mirrors reflect?   some   all

79. Are some / all people living in Australia?   some   all

80. Do some / all microscopes magnify?   some   all

I.E.P. Goal: The client will answer Some/All Questions with 90% or greater accuracy.

Question Comprehension
Task I: True/False Statements

Circle true or false to answer each question.   The first one is done for you.

1. A snail can go as fast as a rabbit.   true   (false)

2. Fish can walk on the beach.   true   false

3. A bookcase can be full of books.   true   false

4. You can eat soup with a spoon.   true   false

5. You can see through a window.   true   false

6. People have two paws.   true   false

7. Saturday and Sunday fall on a weekend.   true   false

8. Mechanics can fix car engines.   true   false

9. Paper is made from wood.   true   false

10. A telephone can have a busy signal.   true   false

11. A book can read.   true   false

12. Kings and queens live in castles.   true   false

13. A calendar tells everyone the time of day.   true   false

14. A spatula is used to pick up warm cookies from a cookie sheet.   true   false

15. A carpenter uses wood in his work.   true   false

16. A chemist works in a laboratory.   true   false

17. To sew something together is to mend.   true   false

18. Baseball players belong to a league.   true   false

19. A crooked line is not straight.   true   false

20. November comes before December.   true   false

21. A chicken can get chicken pox.   true   false

22. A diving board is under the water.   true   false

23. It becomes night after the day.   true   false

24. Colorado is the name of a city.   true   false

25. Spaghetti is an Italian food.   true   false

26. You should believe whatever you are told.   true   false

27. A butterfly was once a caterpillar.   true   false

28. Guitarists like to strum their guitars.   true   false

29. A cricket is a type of flower.   true   false

30. Farmers irrigate their fields.   true   false

31. A fish has scales to weigh himself.   true   false

32. A dinosaur is a prehistoric animal.   true   false

33. You have to blow to make a harp work.   true   false

34. On Halloween, everyone has an Easter Egg Hunt.   true   false

35. A cathedral is a type of church.   true   false

36. You might see an acrobat at the circus.   true   false

37. A cowboy rides a cow to the office.   true   false

38. To reach England, you would need to take a ship or plane.   true   false

39. Alaska is north of the equator.   true   false

40.	A bassinet goes with a baby.	true	false
41.	The radius of a circle is longer than the diameter.	true	false
42.	Cold water will sterilize a glass.	true	false
43.	Submarines can go many fathoms.	true	false
44.	A jockey rides thoroughbreds for a living.	true	false
45.	A microscope minimizes everything.	true	false
46.	Cardboard is made from plastic.	true	false
47.	Opera is a type of musical instrument.	true	false
48.	To pretend to be someone you're not is to impersonate.	true	false
49.	A washing machine agitates.	true	false
50.	A Portuguese Man of War is a soldier from Portugal.	true	false

I.E.P. Goal: The client will answer true/false questions with 90% or greater accuracy.

Question Comprehenson
Task J: *Always/Sometimes/Never* Statements

Circle the correct word to make each sentence true.   The first one is done for you.

1. A television set (always / sometimes / never) has a picture tube.

2. A telephone (always / sometimes / never) has a busy signal.

3. A sailboat (always / sometimes / never) has an engine.

4. People (always / sometimes / never) sit down to eat their lunches.

5. Fish (always / sometimes / never) live in the water.

6. A library (always / sometimes / never) has books.

7. A suit (always / sometimes / never) has a jacket.

8. A man (always / sometimes / never) has a mustache.

9. A shirt (always / sometimes / never) has buttons.

10. A book (always / sometimes / never) has pages.

11. Shoes (always / sometimes / never) have buckles.

12. You (always / sometimes / never) put your coat on before your shirt.

13. You can (always / sometimes / never) see the sun in the daytime.

14. You would (always / sometimes / never) wear a fur coat in the summertime.

15. A bicycle (always / sometimes / never) has three wheels.

16. A clock (always / sometimes / never) tells you the time.

17. A waterfall (always / sometimes / never) has a rainbow.

18. A dictionary (always / sometimes / never) has words.

19. A dog (always / sometimes / never) has long hair.

20. Mothers are (always / sometimes / never) women.

21. The sun (always / sometimes / never) goes down when the day is done.

22. Apples are (always / sometimes / never) red.

23. Carrots (always / sometimes / never) grow on trees.

24. A horse is (always / sometimes / never) an animal.

25. A building is (always / sometimes / never) tall.

26. A window will (always / sometimes / never) open.

27. A race (always / sometimes / never) has a finish line.

28. Women (always / sometimes / never) marry.

29. Shirts are (always / sometimes / never) white.

30. Bananas are (always / sometimes / never) yellow vegetables.

31. Children are (always / sometimes / never) well behaved.

32. An army (always / sometimes / never) has soldiers.

33. Doctors are (always / sometimes / never) men.

34. Reporters (always / sometimes / never) sing their newscasts.

35. Sandwiches are (always / sometimes / never) food.

36. The wind (always / sometimes / never) blows in the winter.

37. Mathematics (always / sometimes / never) involves numbers.

38. Weekends are (always / sometimes / never) four days long.

39. Houses (always / sometimes / never) have a basement.

40. Waves are (always / sometimes / never) made of water.

41. The sun is (always / sometimes / never) hot.

42. Husbands are (always / sometimes / never) married.

43. Bracelets are (always / sometimes / never) worn on the wrists.

44. A kindergarten (always / sometimes / never) has children.

45. A tree (always / sometimes / never) has roots.

46. People are (always / sometimes / never) happy.

47. Children (always / sometimes / never) cry.

48. Beaches (always / sometimes / never) have cattle.

49. A dog (always / sometimes / never) has hooves.

50. Movies are (always / sometimes / never) made on film.

51. Stars (always / sometimes / never) have five points.

52. Colleges are (always / sometimes / never) institutions of higher learning.

53. A quarterback (always / sometimes / never) plays with a basketball during the game.

54. Rugs are (always / sometimes / never) gold.

55. Bottles are (always / sometimes / never) made of plastic.

56. Buses (always / sometimes / never) provide transportation.

57. Trucks (always / sometimes / never) have freight.

58. Volcanos (always / sometimes / never) erupt.

59. Apartments (always / sometimes / never) have tenants.

60. Locks (always / sometimes / never) open with keys.

61. Whales are (always / sometimes / never) mammals.

62. Trains (always / sometimes / never) run on tracks.

63. Countries are (always / sometimes / never) democratic.

64. Neighbors are (always / sometimes / never) friendly.

65. Iron is (always / sometimes / never) a mineral.

66. Women are (always / sometimes / never) female.

67. Dentists are (always / sometimes / never) concerned with dental hygiene.

68. Hair is (always / sometimes / never) auburn.

69. The Olympics (always / sometimes / never) have athletes.

70. Ferris wheels (always / sometimes / never) rotate.

71. People (always / sometimes / never) have dimples.

72. When it is cloudy it (always / sometimes / never) rains.

73. Good friends (always / sometimes / never) reciprocate favors.

74. A cave (always / sometimes / never) contains hieroglyphics.

75. Students (always / sometimes / never) matriculate.

76. The skin (always / sometimes / never) has pores.

77. Children (always / sometimes / never) mature as they get older.

78. Church services should (always / sometimes / never) be reverent.

79. People should (always / sometimes / never) embezzle.

80. A duck is (always / sometimes / never) an amphibian.

I.E.P. Goal: The client will choose the correct word to complete a sentence including the words "always", "sometimes" or "never" with 90% or greater accuracy.

Question Comprehension: General Activities

1. Collect objects to compare their various characteristics (i.e., length, weight, temperature, height, etc.).   Ask the student to choose two objects, and ask him a comparative question about the two objects (e.g., Which is longer - the toothpick or the ruler?).   Keep note of the questions used, asking the same questions without the objects in sight following this activity or on a subsequent day, referring to how the objects looked or felt, as necessary for cueing.

2. Give each student a picture of a different object or animal.   Instruct the students that they are to become their picture.   State what each child is and ask *Can*-Questions to each student as related to his picture (e.g., You are a bird.   Can you sing?; You are a kettle.   Can you sleep?).   Then collect the pictures and ask *If*-Questions employing the same concepts as in the *Can*-Questions previously used (e.g., If you were a bird, could you sing?; If you were a kettle, could you sleep?).

3. Using pictures cut from magazines or catalogs, practice concepts of quantity or comparison.   Label two envelopes with different price ranges (e.g., more than $100.00 and less than $100.00).   Ask the student to take a picture from the stack, placing it in the appropriate envelope.   Begin with items that are easily discernable (e.g., chewing gum, a car, a pencil, a house) and progress to items that are more difficult to decide the price range (e.g., tires, a radio, a coat, etc.).   After practice has been done with this concept with a variety of objects, ask questions for quantity and comparison without using the pictures (e.g., "Which costs more, a television or a pair of socks?").

4. Ask the student *Always/Sometimes/Never* Questions as they pertain to himself.   Ask questions regarding characteristics that will remain constant, those that will change, and those which could never apply to the student.
    Examples: Is your name Ann Marie? (always)
             Are you a female? (always)
             Are you ten years old? (sometimes)
             Are you a grandfather? (never)
             Do you wear dresses? (sometimes)
             Do you have blue eyes? (always)
             Do you ride your bicycle to school? (sometimes)
             Do you have three ears? (never)

    As an alternate activity, ask the student to list characteristics about himself that fall in the *always/sometimes/never* categories.   Or students may wish to choose an object, animal, or place and list the *always/sometimes/never* items which apply to each (e.g., shoes are sometimes brown; cats always like to eat fish; Philadelphia is never in Utah).

5. Collect a variety of objects and containers and place them on the table in view of the student.   Without allowing the student to touch the objects, ask questions regarding which of the objects would fit in which of the containers (e.g., Will the pencil fit in the jar?;   Will the yardstick fit in the purse?; Will the book fit in the wallet?).   If the student answers correctly, follow with a *Why*- or *Why Not*-Question.   The goal of

this activity is to get the student to use statements of quantity and comparison. For example: Will the eraser fit in the envelope? (yes)
Why? (because the envelope is larger than the eraser)
Will the book fit in the wallet? (no)
Why not? (because the wallet is smaller than the book)

If the student answers the initial question incorrectly, let the student manipulate the object and the container so that he can determine why his answer was incorrect. Following this activity, ask the same questions used in the activity for quantity and comparison, without a visual presentation.

6. Assemble *Yes/No* Questions commensurate with the age level or skill level of the student or students.   There should be a mixture in terms of the difficulty of questioning and the type of questioning.   A non-verbal response mode is emphasized in this activity, making it extremely adaptable to the post-stroke individual having very limited expressive language.   In response to these *Yes/No* Questions presented aloud, the student will:
   a)   point to a green light/card for *yes* or a red light/card for *no*; or
   b)   raise the hand for *yes* and stamp the foot for *no*; or
   c)   tap once for *yes* and two for *no*; or
   d)   point to the happy face for *yes* and a sad face for *no*.

Any response mode emphasizing a non-verbal response to *Yes/No* Questions would be appropriate.

7. *True/False* Quiz Game - divide the students into equal teams (as many as the number of students and practicality allow).   *True/False* Questions are presented aloud to the first team, which has 10 seconds to respond with a "true" or "false" answer; an accurate response renders 5 points.   If they are incorrect, a new question is presented to the next team.   The team with the most points at the end of the game wins.

8. Present aloud to the student or students a noun and proceed to ask *Yes/No* Questions concerning the placement of this noun in specific categories.   This involves cross-categorical identification skills as well as auditory reception skills.   For example, *policeman*: Does he belong to the category of men? (yes).   Is he a community helper? (yes).   Is he an animal? (no); *vase*: Is it a container? (yes).   Would it be found in the category of "glass"? (yes).   Does it belong to the "cardboard" category? (no); *box*: Is it a container? (yes).   Does it belong to the "glass" category? (no).   Could it be found in the "cardboard" category? (yes).

Association

Association is the process of attaching meaning to stimuli after it has been received by the auditory or visual channel — the synthesizing of material that has been received. It interconnects receptive language concepts, assimilating experiences for future expression.

It may be necessary to supply many visual cues to aid in the formation of verbal associations if the student is particularly weak in this area. These cues, such as the formation of the initial phoneme of the desired response or actually pointing to the object which represents the correct response, should be faded gradually until the student is capable of making an association solely on the basis of auditory or written stimuli.

Remediation of this particular deficit should also be carried out in an environmental context. Such remediation would include questioning the student in regard to daily activities and attempting to relate these activities to past or future experiences, in addition to supplying the appropriate vocabulary for these familiar situations.

Association

Task A: Completion of "If...then" Statements

Finish each sentence.   The first one is done for you.

1. If you cut your finger, then *it will bleed* _____.

2. If it is dark, then _____.

3. If you forget to wear your coat, then _____.

4. If you fell out of a tree, then _____.

5. If your shoe was broken, then _____.

6. If someone says hello to you, then _____.

7. If you are tired, then _____.

8. If it is cold outside, then _____.

9. If you jump into a swimming pool, then _____.

10. If your shoes hurt, then _____.

11. If you are lost, then _____.

12. If you eat a big dinner, then _____.

13. If you break a glass, then _____.

14. If someone finds a dime, then _____.

15. If you forget your friend's phone number, then _____.

16. If it's your birthday, then _____.

17. If your soup is too hot, then _____.

18. If you don't buy gas for the car, then _____.

19. If you didn't do your homework, then _____.

20. If you forget to water your plants, then _____.

21. If you want your friends to come over, then _____.

22. If you unplug the refrigerator, then _____.

23. If an inner tube has a hole in it, then _____.

24. If you have a fever and a cough, then _____.

25. If you forget to take your homework papers out of your pocket,

    then _____.

26. If you forget to put a stamp on a letter before mailing it,

    then _____.

27. If the faucet drips, then _____.

28. If you forget to grease the cake pan, then _____.

29. If you buy sour milk, then _____.

30. If the traffic signal is broken, then _____.

31. If the elevator is stuck in between floors, then _____.

32. If you need to make a phone call but only have a dollar bill,

    then _____.

33. If a football player makes a touchdown, then _____.

34. If someone gives you a gift that is the wrong size, then _____.

35. If you open a camera while the film is still in it, then _____.

36. If you forgot to add detergent to the laundry, then _____.

37. If you don't know the meaning of a word, then _____.

38. If you fell asleep in the sun, then _____.

39. If a horse breaks a leg, then _____.

40. If your watch stops at two o'clock, then _____.

41. If a cake does not rise, then _____.

42. If your flight is overdue, then _____.

43. If your magazine subscription expires, then _____.

44. If it is leap year, then _____.

45. If there is an eclipse, then _____.

46. If a flood warning is in effect, then _____.

47. If your checking account is overdrawn, then _____.

48. If you do not pay your income tax, then _____.

49. If you need a mortgage, then _____.

50. If you want to buy stock, then _____.

I.E.P. Goal: The client will give a logical consequence for an occurrence when presented with an "If...then" statement with 90% or greater accuracy.

Note: This format may have to be taught initially by asking *What*-Questions.
Example: If it rains, then...what will happen?

Association
Task B: Situational Associations with Clues

Read each group of sentences. Then answer the questions. The first one is done for you.

1. I was blowing up a balloon. There was a loud noise. What do you think happened?

   The balloon burst.

2. The tire blew out. The car swerved to the right side of the road. What might happen?

   _____

3. I forgot about the cake. Smoke poured out of the oven. What had happened?

   _____

4. I fell out of a tree. I could not move my arm. What happened?

   _____

5. The neighbor's lights were off. The door was locked. The car was not in the garage. What happened?

   _____

6. The lights went out. The TV stopped working. What happened?

   _____

7. The earth trembled. The house shook and the windows rattled. What happened?

   _____

8. My shoes were new. The floor had just been waxed. I ran to answer the phone. What do you think might happen?

   _____

9. The man was very fat. The chair was old and weak. He sat down. What do you think might happen?

   _____

10. I left my records on the porch. The sun shone brightly and it was very hot. What do you think might happen?

_____

11. The girl screamed and covered her eyes. When she did, her popcorn fell on the floor. Where was she?

_____

12. The green monsters were chasing me. As the alarm clock rang, I opened my eyes and sat up. What had happened?

_____

13. Ellen had never done the laundry. "The more detergent I use, the cleaner the clothes will be," she thought. So she added 4 cups of detergent to the washing machine. What will happen?

_____

14. Mary turned the candle over onto the curtains. They became very hot and smoky. What had happened?

_____

15. The boy parked the car on the hill and left the brake off. What will happen?

_____

16. It was freezing outside and the white things were falling from the sky. What was happening?

_____

17. When the family got home, the front door was wide open and they couldn't find all their furniture. What had happened?

_____

18. The teacher was angry and the boy was sitting on the bench in the principal's office. What had happened?

_____

19. Mark was to make a speech at school tomorrow. He fell asleep before he had started to work on it. What will happen?

_____

20. The score was tied 88-88 when the boy on the red team got the ball in the basket. The buzzer signaling the end of the game went off. What happened?

_____

21. The children were all dressed in funny costumes. They went from door to door with sacks of candy. What was happening?

_____

22. The bush was dry and brown looking. The little girl had forgotten to water it for two months. What had happened?   _____

23. Jerry put some money on the bench in the lunch room. He went back to get it the next day. What had happened?   _____

24. Roger left the freezer door open all day. What happened?   _____

25. The mother left the eggs to boil on the stove all afternoon. What happened?   _____

26. Jason dropped a penny into the pool. What happened?   _____

27. The glue leaked all over the teacher's papers. What happened?   _____

28. Martha turned on the water in the bathtub and left to get the mail. She stopped to talk to a neighbor for thirty minutes. What happened?   _____

29. The man packed his clothes in a hurry. He forgot to check his closet for his shirts. What happened?   _____

30. Dennis forgot to advance the film before he took the next picture. What happened?   _____

I.E.P. Goal: When presented with facts concerning a situation, the client will provide a logical explanation of the occurrence with 90% or greater accuracy.

Association
Task C: Situational Associations for Categorical Items

This is a guessing activity. I'll tell you some things that are found in the same place. Then, you guess the name of the place. Let's try one.

Note: The most obvious clues to bring each situation to mind are indicated by an asterisk (*). The lowest level of difficulty for this task would be presentation of all items in each group. The level of difficulty will increase as the number of items presented is decreased. The highest level of difficulty on this task is the presentation of only two items which are not noted as being the most obvious clues (*).

1. teacher*
   books*
   desk
   ruler
   chalk
   bell   *(school)*

2. cage*
   monkeys*
   elephant
   lion
   reptile house
   feeders   *(zoo)*

3. swings*
   slides*
   benches
   trees
   squirrels
   sidewalks   *(park)*

4. balls*
   bats*
   gloves
   umpire
   bases
   team   *(baseball game)*

5. clown*
   trapeze*
   tent
   peanuts
   elephant
   tiger   *(circus)*

6. bathtub*
   sink*
   towels
   toothbrush
   soap
   water   *(bathroom)*

7. food*
   cash register*
   bag clerk
   carts
   aisles
   boxes   *(grocery store)*

8. sand*
   waves*
   shells
   sun
   bathing suits
   towels   *(beach)*

9. waitress*
   food*
   silverware
   menu
   tables/chairs
   napkins   *(restaurant)*

10. bride*
    church*
    minister
    flower
    ring
    ushers   *(wedding)*

11. Ferris wheel*
    prizes*
    games
    tickets
    merry-go-round
    hot dogs   *(carnival)*

12. floor*
    wall*
    window
    door
    ceiling
    electrical outlets   *(room)*

13. water*
    diving board*
    lifeguard
    safety rope
    kick boards
    steps   *(swimming pool)*

14. paper plates*
    fried chicken*
    lemonade
    tablecloth
    ants
    the park   *(picnic)*

15. glove compartment*
    dashboard*
    steering wheel
    radio
    seats
    doors   *(car/truck)*

16. runway*
    stewardess*
    tower
    waiting area
    loudspeaker
    baggage   *(airport)*

17. players*
    stadium
    helmets
    cheerleaders
    bleachers
    referee   (football game)

18. hoses*
    trucks*
    axes
    alarm
    garage
    boots/hat   (fire station)

19. jelly beans*
    play (plastic) grass*
    chocolate bunnies
    malted eggs
    marshmallow chickens
    basket   (Easter)

20. waiting room*
    medicine*
    nurse
    thermometer
    stethoscope
    chart   (doctor's office)

21. sleeping bags*
    fire*
    tent
    hiking boots
    insect repellant
    s'mores   (camping)

22. books*
    card catalog*
    check-out card
    magazines
    shelves
    copy machine   (library)

23. paint*
    cash register*
    nails
    rakes
    seeds
    locks   (hardware store)

24. mail carrier*
    scales*
    stamps
    envelopes
    slots
    boxes   (post office)

25. mechanic*
    cars*
    wrench
    oil
    spare parts
    tires   (garage)

26. wallet*
    keys*
    mirror
    hairbrush
    tissues
    lipstick   (purse)

27. washers*
    dryers*
    detergent
    change machine
    clothes carts
    washtubs   (laundromat)

28. locker room*
    weights*
    indoor track
    basketball court
    showers
    sauna   (gymnasium)

29. pews*
    altar*
    Bible
    choir
    pulpit
    minister   (church)

30. lanes*
    exits*
    trucks
    highway patrol cars
    billboards
    rest stops   (interstate)

31. conductor*
    orchestra*
    violins
    baton
    cello
    woodwinds   *(concert)*

32. camera*
    producer*
    lights
    actors
    director
    script   *(movie studio)*

33. diploma*
    mortarboard*
    parents
    valedictorian
    procession
    students   *(graduation)*

34. anesthesia*
    scalpel*
    surgeon
    patient
    sutures
    scrub nurse   *(operating room)*

35. Confederacy*
    Union*
    slaves
    soldiers
    Abraham Lincoln
    Appomattox   *(Civil War)*

I.E.P. Goal: The client will identify the place or situation which is brought to mind when presented aloud with two, three, four, five, or six items commonly found in each situation with 90% or greater accuracy.

Association
Task D: Changing Sentences to Have Opposite Meanings

Read each sentence. Then, rewrite the sentence changing each underlined word to its opposite. The first one is done for you.

1. Go <u>inside</u> now. _Go outside now._ _____

2. I was the <u>first</u> one in line. _____

3. The man is very <u>thin</u>. _____

4. Raise your <u>left</u> hand. _____

5. The grapes taste <u>sour</u>. _____

6. The sweater is too <u>loose</u>. _____

7. The cookie jar is <u>empty</u>. _____

8. The ice is <u>smooth</u> today. _____

9. Yesterday, I was <u>late</u> for school. _____

10. That train is very <u>noisy</u>. _____

11. Is the box <u>heavy</u>? _____

12. That hammock looks very weak. _____

13. Crooked trees are on either side of the road. _____

14. The football field is enormous. _____

15. I left home at two o'clock. _____

16. I sold four boxes of cookies. _____

17. Your answer is incorrect. _____

18. This problem is difficult. _____

19. We import a lot of food. _____

20. They seldom visit our neighborhood. _____

21. The towel is wet and soft. _____

22. The rabbit was quick and smart. _____

23. The wealthy man drove a new car. _____

24. The pencil is long and sharp. _____

25. Old songs are the best songs. _____

26. Can you go over the low fence? _____

27. Heavy pans cost the most. _____

28. The bracelet is old and dull. _____

29. The girl's skin was very smooth. _____

30. The curvy road was lightly traveled. _____

31. The large dog was very ferocious. _____

32. The new dress is very fancy. _____

33. He hit the baseball on his last try. _____

34. I was awake before the snowstorm. _____

35. Friends are honest. _____

36. The boy who sits in <u>front</u> of me is <u>fat</u>. _____

37. I said <u>hello</u> to the <u>last girl</u> in line. _____

38. <u>Early</u> in the <u>morning</u> the house is noisy. _____

39. We could see the <u>dark</u> sky
    <u>below</u> us as we flew <u>over</u>. _____

40. The <u>man's wife</u> is my <u>aunt</u>. _____

I.E.P. Goal: Given a sentence, the client will change identified words to opposites so the sentence has an opposite meaning with 90% or greater accuracy.

Association
Task E: Perceiving and Correcting Nonsense in Sentences

These sentences don't make sense.   Rewrite each sentence so it makes sense.   The first one is done for you.

1. Always put on your jeans before your underwear.

    Always put on your underwear before your jeans. _____

2. The car is almost out of gas; please stop at the hospital.

    _____

3. I got dried and then I took a shower.

    _____

4. When I dropped the carton of eggs, the skins broke.

    _____

5. The florist told me that I should brush my teeth daily.

    _____

6. The ice cream froze in the hot sun.

    _____

7. Last week at school, the clown assigned us a lot of homework.

    _____

8. Grandparents can't listen to the radio without their glasses.

    _____

9. In the fall, the buds fall off the trees.

_____

10. I stubbed my elbow because I was wearing my sandals.

_____

11. The boys were able to see the baseball game with their headphones.

_____

12. Mark put in a new light bulb which made the room dark.

_____

13. The police officer blew his finger to stop the traffic.

_____

14. At the swimming pool, there is a lifeguard's chair and a diving tree.

_____

15. Mr. Stewart asked the waitress to check under the hood.

_____

16. The hardware store was out of apples.

_____

17. The football team won the game by scoring ten baskets.

_____

18. When the light bulb burned out, I replaced the fuse.

_____

19. Because I used suntan lotion, I got a sunburn.

_____

20. The new radiators were working well, putting out cold air.

_____

21. The typewriter typed from right to left.

_____

22. The club elected Sam as their king.

_____

23. The artist thins his paints with honey.

_____

24. Last week, I saw a penny fall up the grate.

_____

25. The building fell down because it was tired.

_____

26. The envelope bounced down the steps and rolled out the door.

_____

27. Our church has 25 people singing in the band.

_____

28. The hockey player was benched for throwing his racquet at a player.

_____

29. The mother of the bride was so happy she cried during the entire funeral.

_____

30. The fire was too hot, so I threw some more wood on it.

_____

I.E.P. Goal: The client will identify inappropriate or nonsensical elements in sentences with 90% or greater accuracy.

Association
Task F: Object Comparison for Similarities and Differences

Read each pair of words.   Then, write one way they are the same, and one way they are different.   The first one is done for you.

1. cow   *same*   They both are farm animals.

   pig   *different*   A pig is smaller than a cow.

2. dog   *same*   _____

   cat   *different*   _____

3. milk   *same*   _____

     orange juice   *different*   _____

4. green beans   *same*   _____

     peas   *different*   _____

5. toes   *same*   _____

     fingers   *different*   _____

6. television   *same*   _____

     radio   *different*   _____

7. taxicab   *same*   _____

     car   *different*   _____

8. table   *same*   _____

     desk   *different*   _____

9. jar   *same*   _____

     box   *different*   _____

10. shoe   *same*   _____

     sock   *different*   _____

11. sun   *same*   _____

     lamp   *different*   _____

12. ring   *same*   _____

     bracelet   *different*   _____

13. chalk   *same*   _____

     pen   *different*   _____

14. clock   *same*   _____

     watch   *different*   _____

15. roller skates   *same*   _____

     ice skates   *different*   _____

16. yarn   *same*   _____

     rope   *different*   _____

17. needle   *same*   _____

     pin   *different*   _____

18. couch   *same*   _____

     bed   *different*   _____

19. raft   *same*   _____

     inner tube   *different*   _____

20. suitcase   *same*   _____

     purse   *different*   _____

21. envelope   *same*   _____

     sheet of paper   *different*   _____

22. camel   *same*   _____

     horse   *different*   _____

23. curtains   *same*   _____

     bedspread   *different*   _____

24. scissors   *same*   _____

     pliers   *different*   _____

25. eggbeater   *same*   _____

     electric mixer   *different*   _____

26. graham cracker   *same*   _____

     Oreo cookie   *different*   _____

27. calculator   *same*   _____

     adding machine   *different*   _____

28. typewriter   *same*   _____

     printing press   *different*   _____

29. telephone book   *same*   _____

    dictionary   *different*   _____

30. novel   *same*   _____

    play   *different*   _____

I.E.P. Goal: The client will correctly give one similarity and one difference for two nouns with 90% or greater accuracy.

Association
Task G: Positive/Negative Descriptions

I. Circle all the correct answers for each positive/negative description.   The first one is done for you.

1. What is fast, but not big?

    jet   (bee)   snail   (mouse)   horse   (rabbit)

2. What is strong, but not sharp?

    pin   axe   rope   cage   net   thread

3. What is noisy, but not heavy?

    bulldozer   whistle   cricket   car   train   alarm clock

4. What rips, but cannot stretch?

    sweater   cotton cloth   paper   bag   fingernail   sock

5. What melts, but is not cold?

    ice   wax   wood   plastic   crayon   Popsicle

6. What is big, but not heavy?

    truck   poster   cloud   brick   dresser   aircraft

7. What floats, but is not light?

    log   ship   leaf   car   bicycle   wind

8. What moves, but does not have a motor?

    airplane   snake   car   bicycle   wind   river

9. What is round, but not light?

    penny   planet   balloon   tire   plate   bowling ball

10. What breaks, but is not glass?

     stick   plate   balloon   watch   mirror   person's leg

11. What bends, but is not metal?

     paper clip   elbow   nail   wire   tree   rubber band

12. What sticks, but is not liquid?

     honey   door   glue   tape   stamp   tree sap

13. What flies, but does not walk?

     airplane   duck   balloon   bird   kite   person

14. What grows, but does not get taller?

     tree   fingernail   moss   grass   hair   savings account

15. What rolls, but does not bounce?

     marble   ball   wheel   dog   tide   rolling pin

I.E.P. Goal: The client will indicate which object fits the positive/negative description with 90% or greater accuracy.

II. Write two things that fit each description.   The first one is done for you.

1. What closes, but does not lock?   *mouth*   *book*

2. What shines, but does not get hot?   _____ _____

3. What do we chew, but do not swallow?   _____ _____

4. What floats, but cannot swim?   _____ _____

5. What is liquid, but is not to drink?   _____ _____

6. What breaks, but does not crumble?   _____ _____

7. What can we raise that we cannot plant?   _____ _____

8. What moves, but is not alive?   _____ _____

9. What can be folded, but cannot be ripped?   _____ _____

10. What can we hear, but cannot see?   _____ _____

11. What can we see, but cannot touch?   _____ _____

12. What smells good, but does not taste good?   _____ _____

13. What can be turned up, but does not get hotter?   _____ _____

14. What is slippery, but is not wet?   _____ _____

15. What runs, but does not have feet?   _____ _____

16. What can be cut, but cannot be glued back
    together?   _____ _____

17. What can be brushed, but cannot be combed?   _____ _____

18. What is round, but does not bounce?   _____ _____

19. What is sharp, but is not pointed?   _____ _____

20. What can we catch, but cannot throw?   _____ _____

I.E.P. Goal: The client will generate at least one appropriate item which fits a positive/negative description with 90% or greater accuracy.

Association
Task H: Rhyming Riddles

This is a guessing activity that gives you some clues about a word. One clue will be a word that rhymes with the answer. Write the answer. The first one is done for you.

1. It rhymes with *long*. It is something that is sung.   _*song*_

2. It rhymes with *couch*. We say this when we get hurt.   _____

3. It rhymes with *inch*. It hurts when someone does this to us.   _____

4. It rhymes with *preacher*. This person is found in a classroom.   _____

5. It rhymes with *go*. It means the opposite of fast.   _____

6. It rhymes with *light*. It is the opposite of day.   _____

7. It rhymes with *drunk*. This animal does not smell very good.   _____

8. It rhymes with *shape*. It is a small, green fruit.   _____

9. It rhymes with *dream*. These lines are on the sides of our
   pants.   _____

10. It rhymes with *tough*. Sandpaper feels this way.   _____

11. It rhymes with *bear*. It means the same as rip.   _____

12. It rhymes with *sport*. Tennis players play on one.   _____

13. It rhymes with *clock*.   Ships tie up at one of these.   _____

14. It rhymes with *raise*.   Cattle do this in the pasture.   _____

15. It rhymes with *sorrow*.   We do this when we get a loan.   _____

16. It rhymes with *puddle*.   Football players gather in one.   _____

17. It rhymes with *now*.   Farmers use it to till the earth.   _____

18. It rhymes with *carriage*.   It takes place when a couple weds.   _____

19. It rhymes with *brace*.   It means to draw over something.   _____

20. It rhymes with *care*.   Selfish people do not do this.   _____

21. It rhymes with *beat*.   Students who are not honest do this.   _____

22. It rhymes with *Psalm*.   It means the same as peaceful.   _____

23. It rhymes with *grow*.   It is the opposite of an amateur.   _____

24. It rhymes with *facts*.   The government takes this from our income.   _____

25. It rhymes with *bugs*.   They spark and are found in an engine.   _____

I.E.P. Goal: When presented with a rhyming word and a descriptive phrase in the form of a riddle, the client will answer the riddle with a rhyming word with 90% or greater accuracy.

Note: If the student is having difficulty completing this section, it may be beneficial to review the sections on generation of rhyming words and discrimination of rhyming words in Chapter One: Auditory Discrimination.

Association
Task I: Creating Compound Words

Think of another word to put before or after each of these words.   Write the two words together to make a compound word.   The first one is done for you.

1. air	_airplane_	8. life	_____
2. boat	_____	9. bed	_____
3. sun	_____	10. eye	_____
4. school	_____	11. check	_____
5. sand	_____	12. book	_____
6. door	_____	13. rain	_____
7. yard	_____	14. key	_____

15. shoe	_____	23. man	_____
16. gun	_____	24. foot	_____
17. fish	_____	25. bag	_____
18. moon	_____	26. night	_____
19. nose	_____	27. hair	_____
20. bull	_____	28. hand	_____
21. ship	_____	29. buck	_____
22. father	_____	30. grand	_____

I.E.P. Goal: When given a word, the client will add another word to it in order to form a compound word with 90% or greater accuracy.

Association
Task J: Action-Agent

Write the correct answers to the following questions about actions.   The first one is done for you.

I.   Animal Sounds

1. What barks?	*dog*	14. What hums?	_____
2. What quacks?	_____	15. What baas?	_____
3. What meows?	_____	16. What coos?	_____
4. What sings?	_____	17. What howls?	_____
5. What buzzes?	_____	18. What croaks?	_____
6. What moos?	_____	19. What caws?	_____
7. What oinks?	_____	20. What squeals?	_____
8. What roars?	_____	21. What crows?	_____
9. What neighs?	_____	22. What chatters?	_____
10. What growls?	_____	23. What bleats?	_____
11. What chirps?	_____	24. What brays?	_____
12. What hoots?	_____	25. What lows?	_____
13. What clucks?	_____		

II. Animal Actions

1. What swims? _fish_
2. What flies? _____
3. What stings? _____
4. What hops? _____
5. What gallops? _____
6. What pecks? _____
7. What crawls? _____
8. What bucks? _____
9. What slithers? _____
10. What prances? _____

11. What grazes? _____
12. What pollinates? _____
13. What roosts? _____
14. What waddles? _____
15. What molts? _____
16. What hibernates? _____
17. What coils? _____
18. What soars? _____
19. What roots? _____
20. What burrows? _____

III. Common Nouns

1. What bounces? _ball_
2. What cuts? _____
3. What breaks? _____
4. What rocks? _____
5. What pops? _____
6. What shoots? _____
7. What shines? _____
8. What drips? _____
9. What melts? _____
10. What runs? _____
11. What rings? _____
12. What sails? _____
13. What smells? _____
14. What rips? _____

15. What rolls? _____
16. What burns? _____
17. What freezes? _____
18. What blows? _____
19. What cooks? _____
20. What opens? _____
21. What hangs? _____
22. What spins? _____
23. What folds? _____
24. What cleans? _____
25. What slams? _____
26. What blooms? _____
27. What pounds? _____
28. What stretches? _____

29. What flows? _____
30. What floats? _____
31. What bends? _____
32. What sinks? _____
33. What sways? _____
34. What explodes? _____
35. What turns? _____
36. What wrinkles? _____
37. What cracks? _____
38. What signals? _____
39. What stains? _____
40. What joins? _____
41. What erupts? _____
42. What shocks? _____
43. What flips? _____
44. What stitches? _____
45. What sticks? _____
46. What flattens? _____
47. What clangs? _____
48. What sees? _____
49. What increases? _____

50. What continues? _____
51. What quenches? _____
52. What reverses? _____
53. What restricts? _____
54. What sterilizes? _____
55. What blots? _____
56. What braces? _____
57. What ascends? _____
58. What pivots? _____
59. What accelerates? _____
60. What spans? _____
61. What ceases? _____
62. What seeps? _____
63. What ignites? _____
64. What tills? _____
65. What warps? _____
66. What illuminates? _____
67. What fluctuates? _____
68. What tolls? _____
69. What billows? _____
70. What disintegrates? _____

I.E.P. Goal: When given a question involving an action, the client will give an agent commonly associated with that action with 90% or greater accuracy.

Task K: Agent-Action

I. People

Write what each person does. The first one is done for you.

1. What does a baby do? <u>*cries*</u>

2. What does a boxer do? _____

3. What does a soldier do? _____

4. What does a barber do? _____

5. What does an artist do? _____

6. What does a ballerina do? _____

7. What does a chef do? _____

8. What does a repairman do? _____

9. What does a pilot do? _____

10. What does a farmer do? _____

11. What does a police officer do? _____

12. What does a maid do? _____

13. What does a dentist do? _____

14. What does an actor do? _____

15. What does a doctor do? _____

16. What does a minister do? _____

17. What does a waitress do? _____

18. What does a musician do? _____

19. What does a chauffeur do? _____

20. What does a secretary do? _____

21. What does a tailor do? _____

22. What does a carpenter do? _____

23. What does a professor do? _____

24. What does an architect do? _____

25. What does a king do? _____

26. What does a jockey do? _____

27. What does a porter do? _____

28. What does a lawyer do? _____

29. What does a senator do? _____

30. What does a general do? _____

I.E.P. Goal: When given a name or occupation in the form of a question, the client will name an action commonly performed by that person with 90% or greater accuracy.

II. Objects

Write what each does. The first one is done for you.

1. What does a door do? ___*opens*___

2. What does a pair of scissors do? _____

3. What does a stove do? _____

4. What does a ball do? _____

5. What does an airplane do? _____

6. What does a fan do? _____

7. What does a bell do? _____

8. What does a pencil do? _____

9. What does a crayon do? _____

10. What does a telephone do? _____

11. What does a whistle do? _____

12. What does a flower do? _____

13. What does a bar of soap do? _____

14. What does tape do? _____

15. What does a lawn mower do? _____

16. What does a boat do? _____

17. What does a needle do? _____

18. What does a scale do? _____

19. What does a towel do? _____

20. What does a clock do? _____

21. What does a heart do? _____

22. What does a tractor do? _____

23. What does a candle do? _____

24. What does a razor do? _____

25. What does a wrench do? _____

26. What does medicine do? _____

27. What does a microscope do? _____

28. What does a helmet do? _____

29. What does a microphone do? _____

30. What does a pendulum do? _____

I.E.P. Goal: *When given the name of an object, the client will name an action commonly associated with the object with 90% or greater accuracy.*

Association
Task L: Noun Comparisons for Range of Characteristics

Answer these questions comparing two things.   The first one is started for you.

1. bear   Which one has a trunk?   *elephant*

   elephant   Which one has sharp claws?   *bear*

                 Which one lives in a cave?   _____

                 Which one do people ride?   _____

                 Which one cannot live in a cold climate? _____

2. tree   Which one is taller?   _____

   flower   Which one can a squirrel live in?   _____

                 Which one do bees pollinate?   _____

                 Which one is found in a bouquet?   _____

                 Which one is used to make furniture?   _____

3. lake   Which one would have a boat dock?   _____

   ocean   Which one has shells?   _____

                 Which one is deeper?   _____

                 Which one has tides?   _____

                 Which one has fresh water?   _____

4. pizza   Which one is served hot?   _____

   chocolate cake   Which one do we eat for dessert?   _____

                 Which one goes with spaghetti?   _____

                 Which one is sweeter?   _____

                 Which one is spicier?   _____

5. rocking chair   Which one is usually found in the dining room?   _____

   table   Which one is usually found in a classroom?   _____

                 Which one would you not set a glass of water on?   _____

                 Which one do you play Ping-Pong on?   _____

                 Which one may have an extra leaf?   _____

6. drum   Which one do we beat?   _____

   bugle   Which one has a mouthpiece.   _____

                 Which one can carry a tune?   _____

                 Which one is a percussion instrument?   _____

                 Which one plays in the brass section?   _____

7. book   Which one is heavier?   _____

    magazine   Which one has the most pages?   _____

    Which one has advertisements in it?   _____

    Which one is divided into chapters?   _____

    Which one has current events in it?   _____

8. sweater   Which one has a place to wear a belt?   _____

    jeans   Which one usually has pockets in the back?   _____

    Which one covers your elbows?   _____

    Which one fades when it is washed?   _____

    Which one can be cut off to make something else?   _____

9. pen   Which one usually has an eraser on it?   _____

    pencil   Which one is usually made partly from wood?   _____

    Which one smears easily when it is used?   _____

    Which one stains our clothing?   _____

    Which one is used for signing important documents?   _____

10. apple   Which one grows under the ground?   _____

    potato   Which one might be found in fruit salad?   _____

    Which one might be used to make a pie?   _____

    Which one has eyes?   _____

    Which one is not eaten raw?   _____

I.E.P. Goal: *Given two items, the client will answer questions comparing a range of characteristics for these two items with 90% or greater accuracy.*

Task M: Comparison of Items

Underline the answers to these questions comparing things. The first one is done for you.

I. Comparison of items (groups)

1. Which is bigger?

elephant	<u>house</u>
kitten	<u>lion</u>
<u>bicycle</u>	ant
shoe	<u>canoe</u>
<u>chain</u>	piece of thread

2. Which is colder?

sun	ice
Popsicle	toast
coffee	lemonade
pool	oven
rain	snow

3. Which is louder?

bell	siren
whisper	scream
train	car
tap shoes	sneakers
earthquake	firecracker

4. Which is longer?

arm	leg
belt	watchband
football field	parking space
pencil	needle
yardstick	match

5. Which is stronger?

bear	man
cardboard box	cage
banana peel	eggshell
rope	string
glass	metal

6. Which is easier to do?

draw a circle	write your name
cook a hot dog	bake a cake
dial a telephone	play the piano
give a party	go to a party
paint the walls	scrub the floor

7. Which is heavier?

meat loaf	bed
chair	table
pie	whipped cream
pencil	stamp
brick	brush

8. Which is sharper?

knife	spoon
hammer	saw
pencil	crayon
tooth	tongue
roller skates	ice skates

9. Which is thicker?

thumb	little finger
piece of bologna	slice of toast
whipped cream	orange juice
wire	yarn
comic book	dictionary

10. Which is more expensive?

fur coat	plastic raincoat
yo-yo	skateboard
radio	television
airplane	car
china plate	paper plate

II. Comparison of two items

1. Which is prettier?	butterfly	roach
2. Which is smaller?	feet	hands
3. Which is happier?	clown	sick person
4. Which is meaner?	witch	baby
5. Which is more fun?	school	circus
6. Which is tastier?	ice cream cone	liver
7. Which is smaller?	bobcat	kitten
8. Which is wiser?	dog	man
9. Which person is sicker?	someone with a cold	someone with the flu
10. Which is stickier?	paint	glue
11. Which is older?	grandparent	boy
12. Which is softer?	record	pillow
13. Which is scarier?	ghost	pony
14. Which is cleaner?	mud puddle	towel
15. Which is wetter?	water	dirt
16. Which is more expensive?	boat	house
17. Which do you like better?	toy spider	real spider
18. Which is warmer?	tent	cabin
19. Which is harder?	nose	knee

20. Which is slower?	bike	bus
21. Which is quieter?	bee	helicopter
22. Which is harder?	sleeping bag	bed
23. Which is easier to paint?	wall	ceiling
24. Which is hotter?	light bulb	toaster
25. Which is duller?	spatula	axe

III. Comparison of three items

1. Which is softest?	wood	sponge	ice cream
2. Which is hottest?	stove	light bulb	hairdryer
3. Which is lightest?	pencil	book	stamp
4. Which is heaviest?	chair	lamp	book
5. Which is youngest?	boy	police officer	grandmother
6. Which is tallest?	tree	telephone pole	mailbox
7. Which is fastest?	car	ship	jet
8. Which is sweetest?	cracker	cereal	Coke
9. Which is sharpest?	gun	knife	scissors
10. Which is fanciest?	jeans	pajamas	party dress
11. Which is toughest?	ice cream	lettuce	meat
12. Which is crispest?	taffy	potato chip	banana
13. Which is furthest from your house?	London	Miami	Washington, D.C.
14. Which is roughest?	sand	silk	skin
15. Which is cheapest?	gum	socks	magazine
16. Which is slowest?	elephant	ant	dog
17. Which is thickest?	piece of paper	slice of cheese	slice of bread
18. Which is the most shallow?	puddle	lake	ocean

19.	Which is shiniest?	glass	mirror	plastic
20.	Which is the most expensive?	shirt	coat	gloves
21.	Which is the most brittle?	paper	cloth	autumn leaves
22.	Which is the most buoyant?	brick	plastic jug	key
23.	Which is the most transparent?	tissue paper	tin foil	pantyhose
24.	Which is the most efficient?	computer	adding machine	abacus
25.	Which is the most trustworthy?	pickpocket	priest	salesman

IV. Comparison of four items

1.	Which is lightest?	book	envelope	shoe	orange
2.	Which is darkest?	noon	evening	midnight	morning
3.	Which is saltiest?	graham crackers	apples	lettuce	pretzels
4.	Which is crispiest?	hamburger	pudding	boiled egg	corn chip
5.	Which is quietest?	library	bowling alley	factory	nursery school
6.	Which is oldest?	child	adult	teenager	baby
7.	Which is slickest?	ice	grass	sand	dirt
8.	Which is wildest?	horse	parakeet	mouse	bobcat
9.	Which is longest?	commercial	cartoon	movie	preview
10.	Which is stickiest?	nuts	taffy	cheese	popcorn
11.	Which is the most painful?	bruise	cut	broken leg	scratch
12.	Which is roughest?	velvet	cotton	burlap	silk
13.	Which is driest?	toast	grapes	soup	apple
14.	Which is fattest?	dog	pig	cat	raccoon
15.	Which is liveliest?	elephant	cow	kitten	turtle

16.	Which is cleanest?	mud	grease	soap	dust
17.	Which is calmest?	hurricane	tornado	rain	volcano
18.	Which is most ferocious?	seal	woodchuck	leopard	skunk
19.	Which is fastest?	roller coaster	swing	seesaw	bicycle
20.	Which is most nutritious?	candy bar	green beans	cookies	mints

I.E.P. Goal: Given a characteristic in the form of a question, the client will choose the item which exhibits the specific characteristic with 90% or greater accuracy.

Association
Task N: Object Identification (Definitions)

Write the name of the object described in each of these definitions.   The first one is done for you.

1. Babies like to play with these.   *toys*

2. It is round and is found on a car.   _____

3. People drive these.   _____

4. We write on this.   _____

5. We turn this on to watch a program   _____

6. We sleep in it.   _____

7. What shines in the sky.   _____

8. Something that is dialed.   _____

9. A shape that has four corners.   _____

10. Something that opens and shuts.   _____

11. It spins around and cools the air.   _____

12. People keep their money in this.   _____

13. It is round and we put coffee in it.   _____

14. We use this to make ourselves clean.   _____

15. It is found in a store; it goes up and down; it carries people.   _____

16. We open this to let in some air. _____

17. The place where meals are prepared. _____

18. People put their cigarette ashes in these. _____

19. A book that tells us what words mean. _____

20. Where a colony of bees lives. _____

21. What fire hoses are attached to at the scene of the fire. _____

22. The place where two walls meet at an angle. _____

23. A model of the earth showing the oceans and continents. _____

24. A group of certain animals, such as sheep. _____

25. The foam formed by soap and water. _____

26. Cowboys use this for roping animals. _____

27. A book of maps. _____

28. An instrument used for viewing the stars and planets. _____

29. A violent storm originating in the tropics. _____

30. A Greek-letter organization of men. _____

31. A piece of furniture, silverware, etc., made in a former period. _____

32. An official count of the population. _____

33. A device used for lifting an automobile a short distance. _____

34. An official authorized to certify documents. _____

35. Slats laid in overlapping rows used to cover roofs and sides of houses. _____

I.E.P. Goal: When given a definition, the client will identify the object defined with 90% or greater accuracy.

Task O: Free Word Associations

Read each word below. Then, write a word on the blank that goes with the first word. The first one is done for you.

1. socks _____shoes_____

2. snow _____

3. soap _____

4. hammer _____

5. baby _____

6. sun _____

7. doll _____

8. chair _____

9. teacher _____

10. cup _____

11. knife _____

12. bread _____

13. bird _____

14. coat _____

15. cow _____

16. lamp _____

17. lock _____

18. bottle _____

19. grass _____

20. pen _____

21. window _____

22. house _____

23. thread _____

24. smoke _____

25. pajamas _____

26. letter _____

27. iron _____

28. desert _____

29. diamond _____

30. spend _____

31. wild _____

32. over _____

33. yes _____

34. ring _____

35. oil _____

36. march _____

37. holiday _____

38. club _____

39. plant _____

40. dream _____

41. cobbler _____

42. pebble _____

43. easel _____

44. raft _____

45. closet _____

46. space _____

47. form _____   49. loan _____

48. orchard _____   50. blind _____

I.E.P. Goal: The client will supply a word that is commonly associated with a key word with 90% or greater accuracy.

Association
Task P: Choosing Relationships between Words

Read these word pairs. Write an S on the blank if the words mean almost the same thing. Write an O on the blank if the words are opposites.

1. good   bad   _O_   21. pitch   catch   ____

2. glad   mad   ____   22. trick   cheat   ____

3. talk   speak   ____   23. front   rear   ____

4. clean   dirty   ____   24. fast   speedy   ____

5. big   little   ____   25. near   far   ____

6. work   play   ____   26. creep   crawl   ____

7. fast   slow   ____   27. weak   strong   ____

8. buddy   pal   ____   28. girl   female   ____

9. present   gift   ____   29. mad   angry   ____

10. straight   wavy   ____   30. cost   price   ____

11. last   first   ____   31. tardy   late   ____

12. adult   child   ____   32. push   pull   ____

13. windy   breezy   ____   33. rip   tear   ____

14. rough   smooth   ____   34. easy   difficult   ____

15. up   down   ____   35. wash   bathe   ____

16. loud   noisy   ____   36. pull   tug   ____

17. vacation   trip   ____   37. shade   sun   ____

18. sick   ill   ____   38. recess   playtime   ____

19. nice   mean   ____   39. buy   sell   ____

20. cry   laugh   ____   40. give   take   ____

41. sorrowful   cheerful ____

42. slope   incline ____

43. task   chore ____

44. tough   strong ____

45. trap   release ____

46. wager   bet ____

47. cavity   hole ____

48. buff   polish ____

49. broad   narrow ____

50. brag   boast ____

51. horizontal   vertical ____

52. audio   video ____

53. erupt   explode ____

54. want   desire ____

55. hostile   friendly ____

56. fat   obese ____

57. stop   halt ____

58. large   enormous ____

59. reward   punishment ____

60. group   solo ____

61. latitude   longitude ____

62. remember   forget ____

63. scrub   mop ____

64. switch   change ____

65. debit   credit ____

66. liberal   generous ____

67. char   burn ____

68. charge   accuse ____

69. abrupt   sudden ____

70. awkward   graceful ____

71. arrive   depart ____

72. depend   rely ____

73. edge   border ____

74. elder   younger ____

75. faint   weak ____

76. false   counterfeit ____

77. original   new ____

78. negative   positive ____

79. rescue   save ____

80. idle   busy ____

81. change   vary ____

82. disturb   agitate ____

83. veto   accept ____

84. capable   inept ____

85. comrade   associate ____

86. critical   complimentary ____

87. usual   customary ____

88. sincere   false ____

89. sharp   keen ____

90. sense   meaning ____

91. flexible   pliable ____

92. perfect   marred ____

93. suitable appropriate ____

94. style mode ____

95. evade pursue ____

96. masculine feminine ____

97. ailment illness ____

98. opponent ally ____

99. legitimate illegal ____

100. humid wet ____

101. humble proud ____

102. foe enemy ____

103. remainder balance ____

104. port starboard ____

105. mutual common ____

106. match correspond ____

107. hinder advance ____

108. superficial deep ____

109. habitual usual ____

110. gaudy subdued ____

111. garb attire ____

112. fair impartial ____

113. eccentric unconventional ____

114. degrade humiliate ____

115. include omit ____

116. avarice greed ____

117. void empty ____

118. seldom infrequent ____

119. portion entirety ____

120. vat tank ____

I.E.P. Goal: The client will correctly identify the relationship between two words presented with 90% or greater accuracy.

Association
Task Q: Recalling Opposites

Write the opposite for each word below.   The first one is done for you.

1. up   *down*

2. stop   _____

3. in   _____

4. big   _____

5. good   _____

6. night   _____

7. soft   _____

8. boy   _____

9. happy   _____

10. fat   _____

11. inside   _____

12. mother   _____

13. slow   _____

14. open   _____

15. tall   _____

16. hot   _____

17. old   _____

18. wet   _____

19. left   _____

20. over   _____

21. black   _____

22. easy   _____

23. loud   _____

24. lost   _____

25. light   _____

26. rough   _____

27. long   _____

28. far   _____

29. straight   _____

30. asleep   _____

31. man   _____

32. child   _____

33. young   _____

34. heavy   _____

35. nice   _____

36. high   _____

37. sweet   _____

38. first   _____

39. hello   _____

40. right   _____

41. hit   _____

42. sick   _____

43. early   _____

44. rich   _____

45. bottom   _____

46. morning   _____

47. winner   _____

48. strong   _____

49. push   _____

50. few   _____

51. mine   _____

52. shallow   _____

53. above   _____

54. beginning   _____

55. catch   _____

56. love   _____

57. hers   _____

58. give   _____

59. true   _____

60. sharp   _____

61. beautiful   _____

62. start   _____

63. difficult   _____

64. enemy   _____

65. find   _____

66. question   _____

67. marriage   _____

68. follow   _____

69. success   _____

70. heaven   _____

71.	buy	_____	
72.	save	_____	
73.	whisper	_____	
74.	attic	_____	
75.	narrow	_____	
76.	female	_____	
77.	remember	_____	
78.	absent	_____	
79.	float	_____	
80.	rude	_____	
81.	niece	_____	
82.	war	_____	
83.	ceiling	_____	
84.	I	_____	
85.	careful	_____	
86.	life	_____	
87.	teach	_____	
88.	heel	_____	
89.	future	_____	
90.	multiply	_____	
91.	real	_____	
92.	pro	_____	
93.	add	_____	
94.	hide	_____	
95.	mare	_____	
96.	rooster	_____	

97.	filly	_____	
98.	mountain	_____	
99.	best	_____	
100.	bitter	_____	
101.	wise	_____	
102.	agile	_____	
103.	retreat	_____	
104.	innocent	_____	
105.	idle	_____	
106.	include	_____	
107.	coward	_____	
108.	offense	_____	
109.	inhale	_____	
110.	group	_____	
111.	reward	_____	
112.	victory	_____	
113.	often	_____	
114.	slavery	_____	
115.	increase	_____	
116.	liquid	_____	
117.	professional	_____	
118.	wealth	_____	
119.	counterfeit	_____	
120.	scarce	_____	
121.	latitude	_____	
122.	seek	_____	

123. temporary _____

124. encourage _____

125. release _____

126. create _____

127. admit _____

128. debit _____

129. evade _____

130. stationary _____

131. distribute _____

132. conservative _____

133. dangerous _____

134. arrive _____

135. refuse _____

136. despair _____

137. ignite _____

138. accelerate _____

139. conceal _____

140. commence _____

141. stubborn _____

142. native _____

143. generous _____

144. attract _____

145. convict _____

146. introduction _____

147. register _____

148. pedestrian _____

149. novice _____

150. illuminate _____

I.E.P. Goal: The client will supply the opposite for a word with 90% or greater accuracy.

Note: If the client has difficulty with this task, it is recommended that a sentence completion format be used.

Example: big An elephant is big. An ant is _____. (little)
　　　　　　　If something is not big, it is _____. (little)

Association
Task R: Forming Opposites by Adding Prefixes

Write the opposite of each word by adding a prefix to it. The first one is done for you.

1. clean _____*unclean*_____

2. safe _____

3. honest _____

4. trust _____

5. happy _____

6. sure _____

7. correct _____

8. legal _____

9. lock _____

10. agree _____

11. dress _____

12. button _____

13. zip _____

14. obey _____

15. certain _____

16. important _____

17. friendly _____

18. perfect _____

19. clear _____

20. approve _____

21. sane _____

22. expensive _____

23. fiction _____

24. employment _____

25. modest _____

26. sanitary _____

27. continue _____

28. curl _____

29. mature _____

30. pure _____

31. loyal _____

32. content _____

33. interest _____

34. experienced   _____

35. flexible   _____

36. mobile   _____

37. effective   _____

38. steady   _____

39. moderate   _____

40. negotiable   _____

41. desirable   _____

42. cooperative   _____

43. regular   _____

44. reverent   _____

45. relevant   _____

46. reversible   _____

47. tame   _____

48. sufficient   _____

49. partial   _____

50. flammable   _____

I.E.P. Goal: *The client will supply the opposite for a word by adding an appropriate prefix with 90% or greater accuracy.*

Association
Task S: **Sentence Completion for Opposites**

Read each pair of sentences.   Finish the second sentence with a word that means the opposite of the underlined word in the first sentence.

1. John is a <u>boy</u>.   Mary is a ___*girl*___.

2. A rocket goes <u>up</u>.   Rain comes _____.

3. An elephant is <u>big</u>.   A mouse is _____.

4. Fire is <u>hot</u>.   Snow is _____.

5. Marshmallows are <u>soft</u>.   Rocks are _____.

6. The boy in the park was <u>well</u>. A person with a cold is _____.

7. When you greet someone you say <u>hello</u>. When you leave you say _____.

8. With a house, carpets are on the <u>inside</u>. Shutters are on the _____.

9. A turtle is <u>slow</u>. A rabbit is _____.

10. At night we are <u>asleep</u>. During the day we are _____.

11. A green light means <u>go</u>. A red light means _____.

12. A grandmother is <u>old</u>. A baby is _____.

13. It snows in the <u>winter</u>. It gets hot in the _____.

14. If you have money, you are <u>rich</u>. If you have none, you are _____.

15. A rope is <u>fat</u>. A string is _____.

16. In the swimming pool, you are <u>wet</u>. Lying in the sun, you are _____.

17. The children who are here are <u>present</u>. Those who are not are _____.

18. Lemons are <u>sour</u>. Candy is _____.

19. The ground is <u>below</u>. The sky is _____.

20. Sandpaper is <u>rough</u>. Silk is _____.

21. A glass with water in it is <u>full</u>. A glass without water is _____.

22. A plane goes <u>over</u>. A submarine goes _____.

23. A novel is <u>long</u>. A paragraph is _____.

24. A man is a <u>male</u>. A woman is a _____.

25. A puddle is <u>shallow</u>. An ocean is _____.

26. Twins are <u>alike</u>. Cousins are _____.

27. To put together is to <u>add</u>. To take away is to _____.

28. An elephant is <u>clumsy</u>. A ballerina is _____.

29. Walking a tightrope is very dangerous. Swimming with a lifejacket is

    _____.

30. New cars are very expensive. Newspapers are very _____.

31. To spend money is to buy. To receive money for an object is to _____.

32. Dawn is early. Dusk is _____.

33. When an answer is right, it is said to be true. If it is wrong, then it is said to be

    _____.

34. The choir sings in a group. The lead singer sings a _____.

35. Builders construct. Wrecking crews _____.

36. A young child is immature. An adult is _____.

37. Superman is fictional. George Washington was _____.

38. Fairy tales are mythical. History is _____.

39. Space is infinite. Cities are _____.

40. Milk is a liquid. Bread is a _____.

41. Diamonds are scarce. Coal is _____.

42. If you are in favor of something, you are pro. If you are against it, you are

    _____.

43. If someone commits a crime, he is guilty. If he has not committed a crime, he is

    _____.

44. Money is given as a reward. People are sent to prison as a _____.

45. A female horse is a mare. A male horse is a _____.

46. To go toward something is to advance. To move away from something is to

    _____.

47. To begin a task is to commence. To finish a task is to _____.

48. Someone who drives is a <u>motorist</u>. Someone who walks is a _____.

49. Someone who has no experience is a <u>novice</u>. Someone with much experience is an

    _____.

50. Someone born in this country is a <u>native</u>. A visitor from another country is a

    _____.

I.E.P. Goal: *The client will complete a sentence so that it is the opposite in meaning from the model sentence presented with 90% or greater accuracy.*

Association
Task T: Completion of Analogies

Write a word to finish each analogy statement.   The first one is done for you.

1. Pine trees have pine cones; apple trees have ___*apples*___.

2. My nose is for smelling; my eyes are for _____.

3. A truck has wheels; a dog has _____.

4. My ankle is on my leg; my wrist is on my _____.

5. My feet are for walking; my hands are for _____.

6. My wrist has a watch; my finger has a _____.

7. Cotton is white; bananas are _____.

8. A tree has leaves; a flower has _____.

9. Windows have latches; doors have _____.

10. Shoes have laces; pants have _____.

11. A piano has keys; a violin has _____.

12. A boat has a sail; a car has an _____.

13. People have hair; bears have _____.

14. People have nails; animals have _____.

15. A star has five points; a triangle has _____.

16. A plumber fixes pipes; an electrician fixes _____.

17. A ball is round; a door is _____.

18. Nails have heads; pencils have _____.

117

19. Dentists have patients; teachers have _____.

20. Cash registers have numbers; typewriters have _____.

21. Lamps have light bulbs; candles have _____.

22. A church has pews; a school has _____.

23. Bees have a hive; rabbits have a _____.

24. Eyes have eyelids; a stage has a _____.

25. A clock has hours; a calendar has _____.

26. Nurses have needles; mechanics have _____.

27. Children have knapsacks; cars have _____.

28. Legs have shins; jaws have _____.

29. Football fields have goalposts; baseball diamonds have _____.

30. A typewriter makes carbon copies; a camera makes _____.

31. Summer is to hot as winter is to _____.

32. Bacon and eggs are to breakfast as spaghetti is to _____.

33. A magazine is to read as coffee is to _____.

34. Shovel is to dirt as garden hose is to _____.

35. Moon is to night as sun is to _____.

36. Pipe is to smoke as celery is to _____.

37. Girl is to boy as wife is to _____.

38. Fingernails are to hands as toenails are to _____.

39. Taste is to mouth as hear is to _____.

40. Pencil is to paper as chalk is to _____.

41. Cows are to moo as cats are to _____.

42. Sit is to bench as lie down is to _____.

43. Milk is to carton as jelly is to _____.

44. Red is to stop as yellow is to _____.

45. Bedspread is to bed as rug is to _____.

46. Cards are to deal as dice are to _____.

47. Twelve is to number as "d" is to _____.

48. Webs are to spiders as nests are to _____.

49. Shoe is to foot as hat is to _____.

50. Corn is to vegetable as steak is to _____.

51. Dogs are to bark as ducks are to _____.

52. May is to month as Tuesday is to _____.

53. Robin is to bird as salmon is to _____.

54. Lemons are to sour as oranges are to _____.

55. King is to queen as prince is to _____.

56. Dark is to light as new is to _____.

57. Tractor is to farmer as fishing pole is to _____.

58. Cage is to gerbil as aquarium is to _____.

59. Witch is to broom as pirate is to _____.

60. Brussel sprouts are to vegetables as raspberries are to _____.

61. Hot is to cold as empty is to _____.

62. Advertisement is to newspaper as commercial is to _____.

63. Smile is to happy as frown is to _____.

64. Hosiery is to leg as scarf is to _____.

65. Seat is to bicycle as saddle is to _____.

66. Boat is to water as train is to _____.

67. Pilots are to airplanes as astronauts are to _____.

68. Right is to left as happy is to _____.

69. Start is to finish as beginning is to _____.

70. Stove is to kitchen as shower is to _____.

71. Foot is to feet as toe is to _____.

72. Swimming is to pool as tennis is to _____.

73. Paper is to pad as pages are to _____.

74. Barbers are to hair as bakers are to _____.

75. Firecrackers are to July as Christmas tree is to _____.

76. Up is to down as hill is to _____.

77. A drill is to a dentist as a stethoscope is to a _____.

78. Carpenter is to cabinet as bee is to _____.

79. Brush is to teeth as clip is to _____.

80. Ribbon is to package as necktie is to _____.

81. Firework is to red as grape is to _____.

82. Boat is to harbor as bus is to _____.

83. Scissors are to hair as lawn mower is to _____.

84. Uncle is to nephew as aunt is to _____.

85. Mosquito is to insect as bluejay is to _____.

86. Sun is to shine as grass is to _____.

87. Buick is to car as beets are to _____.

88. Chicago is to Illinois as Miami is to _____.

89. Second is to minute as minute is to _____.

90. Trees are to mountain as syrup is to _____.

91. Pipe is to water as power line is to _____.

92. Diamond is to baseball game as rectangle is to _____.

93. A farmer is to a farm as a conductor is to an _____.

94. A painter is to painting as a butcher is to _____.

95. Caterpillar is to butterfly as tadpole is to _____.

96. Tank is to army as ship is to _____.

97. Palm is to hand as sole is to _____.

98. Picture is to wall as cushion is to _____.

99. Paris is to France as Athens is to _____.

100. Baking powder is to biscuit as helium is to _____.

I.E.P. Goal: *The client will complete analogous statements with a 90% or greater accuracy.*

Association: General Activities

1. Tape a series of isolated environmental sounds, asking the student to associate the sound with the correct object as the tape is played (the student should name the object/person/animal which makes the sound heard).   Suggested sounds to be taped:

animal noises	music box
car horn	door slamming
traffic	train
washing machine	crowd noises at football game
ball bouncing	pencil being sharpened
siren	blender/electric mixer
chain rattling	alarm clock ringing
glass breaking	clock ticking
motorcycle	wood being sanded
bell	balloon popping
sewing machine	electric drill
firecracker	water running
zipper	toilet flushing
diving off diving board	cork popping
hammering	lawn mower

people talking, crying, yelling, singing, snoring, whispering, clapping hands, running, snapping fingers, sneezing, coughing, walking, etc.

musical instruments: piano, guitar, drums, cymbals, banjo, bugle, flute, tuba, violin, fiddle, etc.

If the student has difficulty identifying the sounds with auditory presentation only, provide pictures for the student to point to as he hears the sound each makes.

2. Using several of the above sounds recorded in sequence on tape, make up a story to accompany each of these sounds as they occur.

3. Place pictures of various objects or animals on the table.   Ask Action-Agent Questions (e.g., What barks?, What hops?, etc.), having the student point to the correct picture as he states the answer.   Then, have the student repeat the correct answer in a noun + verb format (e.g., A dog barks.).   Using the same pictures, ask Agent-Action Questions (e.g., What does a dog do?, What does a rabbit do?), requiring the student to state the answer or make the appropriate animal sound.

4. Play a chain word association game with several students.   The clinician or a student should think of the first word, and the students in turn must state a word associated with the word used by the previous person.   An example of a word association chain might be: up - down - town - city - traffic - cars.

5. Using pictures on index cards or words printed on index cards which are frequently used to form compound words, have the student match cards by pairs which form compound words. Then have the students choose cards at random and state if it is a compound word. If the student chooses two cards which form a nonsense compound word (e.g., *housecar*), ask the student to give a definition which fits the nonsense word (e.g., a housecar is a car that people live in).

   Have the students make up nonsense compound words and definitions for a homework assignment. Give them some examples to help them begin (e.g., *shoedump* - a place where old shoes are disposed of).

6. Paste pictures of opposite concepts on index cards, or print opposite words on index cards. Place the cards in random order on the table and instruct the student to match the opposite concepts by pairs. As the student becomes proficient at this task, it may be timed with the student attempting to decrease his time on subsequent trials.

7. Present the student with pictures of objects commonly associated with a situation (e.g., sink, stove, dishes) and instruct the student to name the place or situation brought to mind by the group of pictures. To increase the level of difficulty of this task, present only one picture at a time instructing the student to attempt to name the situation with as few pictorial cues as possible.

8. Give the student two objects which have some characteristics in common and some which are different. Instruct the student to name as many similarities and differences as possible. For example, when presented with an apple and a cherry, the student would state: "They are both round. They are both red. Both are fruit. Both contain seeds. The apple is much bigger. The cherry is juicier." Ask leading questions, if necessary, to elicit the appropriate responses (e.g., Are they both the same size?). Encourage the student to feel and look at each object carefully in order to notice similarities and differences.

9. Illustrate consequences of actions using actual objects. For example: drop an egg; put a cracker in water; blow on a lit match; put a drop of bleach on a dark cloth, etc. As you are demonstrating the consequences of these actions, use "If...then" statements (e.g., If I drop this egg, it will break). Following the demonstration, instruct the students to complete "If...then" statements presented aloud which pertain to the activities performed. Give each student an experiment to perform at home (e.g., putting bread in the toaster when it is not plugged in; mailing a letter without a stamp; writing with a pencil which has been dipped in glue) and have them report on the consequences of their actions the following day. Make a list of "If...then" statements from their reports, and ask them to complete these statements when presented aloud. Be sure to assign experiments which are safe for the student to perform unsupervised at home.

10. Supply the first line of a couplet and ask the student to generate the second line, forming a nonsense rhyme. For example, "My dog's so big and fat..."; student's possible response, "He can't even chase a cat" or "A mouse ran across my toe..."; student's possible response, "I jumped and screamed 'Oh no!' " Then ask the student to compose both lines of a nonsense couplet.

Auditory Memory

Auditory memory is the ability to retain, for later use, auditory events which have occurred in the immediate or distant past. Long and short term memory incorporate recognition, content, and sequence factors to encode language skills from which comparisons may be drawn, to which additional information may be added, or from which an individual may generate appropriate syntactical statements concerning the world about him. It is only with this memory core, programmed through the visual and auditory channels, that one can build on past knowledge in order to use it in the future. Stimulation of auditory memory skills in progressively longer units facilitates more complete processing of verbal language materials and, in turn, facilitates ease of use at a later date.

Task A: Recognition Memory for Numbers in a Pattern

Listen to each number pattern I say.   I will repeat part of the pattern.   You say the part I don't say.

I.   Memory of one item in a two-unit sequence

1.   9 - 4;   9 - (4)   16.   4 - 11;   4 - (11)

2.   8 - 7;   8 - (7)   17.   18 - 24;   18 - (24)

3.   10 - 3;   10 - (3)   18.   10 - 93;   10 - (93)

4.   8 - 1;   8 - (1)   19.   33 - 19;   33 - (19)

5.   2 - 5;   2 - (5)   20.   71 - 84;   71 - (84)

6.   3 - 1;   3 - (1)   21.   45 - 6;   45 - (6)

7.   6 - 4;   6 - (4)   22.   97 - 42;   97 - (42)

8.   2 - 10;   2 - (10)   23.   18 - 63;   18 - (63)

9.   1 - 5;   1 - (5)   24.   101 - 57;   101 - (57)

10.   8 - 2;   8 - (2)   25.   43 - 15;   43 - (15)

11.   7 - 6;   7 - (6)   26.   111 - 152;   111 - (152)

12.   16 - 1;   16 - (1)   27.   172 - 103;   172 - (103)

13.   20 - 4;   20 - (4)   28.   83 - 16;   83 - (16)

14.   7 - 3;   7 - (3)   29.   19 - 141;   19 - (141)

15.   5 - 14;   5 - (14)   30.   65 - 132;   65 - (132)

II.   Memory of one item in a three-unit sequence

1.   3 - 5 - 1;   3 - 5 - (1)   5.   8 - 3 - 9;   8 - 3 - (9)

2.   7 - 6 - 8;   7 - 6 - (8)   6.   8 - 4 - 5;   8 - 4 - (5)

3.   2 - 1 - 7;   2 - 1 - (7)   7.   1 - 7 - 3;   1 - 7 - (3)

4.   1 - 4 - 3;   1 - 4 - (3)   8.   3 - 4 - 1;   3 - 4 - (1)

9. 2 - 5 - 7;   2 - 5 - (7)

10. 4 - 9 - 10;   4 - 9 - (10)

11. 7 - 6 - 2;   7 - 6 - (2)

12. 14 - 8 - 21;   14 - 8 - (21)

13. 17 - 12 - 20;   17 - 12 - (20)

14. 10 - 18 - 13;   10 - 18 - (13)

15. 15 - 11 - 3;   15 - 11 - (3)

16. 61 - 93 - 42;   61 - 93 - (42)

17. 96 - 8 - 44;   96 - 8 - (44)

18. 67 - 76 - 14;   67 - 76 - (14)

19. 88 - 11 - 99;   88 - 11 - (99)

20. 50 - 25 - 73;   50 - 25 - (73)

21. 37 - 87 - 43;   37 - 87 - (43)

22. 81 - 63 - 27;   81 - 63 - (27)

23. 55 - 19 - 102;   55 - 19 - (102)

24. 52 - 64 - 41;   52 - 64 - (41)

25. 103 - 91 - 145;   103 - 91 - (145)

26. 111 - 157 - 188;   111 - 157 - (188)

27. 43 - 100 - 91;   43 - 100 - (91)

28. 128 - 114 - 102;   128 - 114 - (102)

29. 133 - 189 - 95;   133 - 189 - (95)

30. 89 - 121 - 183;   89 - 121 - (183)

III. Memory of one item in a four-unit sequence

1. 9 - 4 - 2 - 8;   9 - 4 - 2 - (8)

2. 1 - 5 - 6 - 2;   1 - 5 - 6 - (2)

3. 7 - 4 - 3 - 1;   7 - 4 - 3 - (1)

4. 6 - 9 - 2 - 4;   6 - 9 - 2 - (4)

5. 4 - 3 - 7 - 8;   4 - 3 - 7 - (8)

6. 3 - 7 - 5 - 2;   3 - 7 - 5 - (2)

7. 9 - 4 - 1 - 3;   9 - 4 - 1 - (3)

8. 2 - 8 - 5 - 7;   2 - 8 - 5 - (7)

9. 8 - 3 - 7 - 9;   8 - 3 - 7 - (9)

10. 5 - 8 - 2 - 10;   5 - 8 - 2 - (10)

11. 7 - 9 - 6 - 2;   7 - 9 - 6 - (2)

12. 6 - 4 - 1 - 3;   6 - 4 - 1 - (3)

13. 3 - 9 - 7 - 1;   3 - 9 - 7 - (1)

14. 8 - 7 - 4 - 6;   8 - 7 - 4 - (6)

15. 6 - 5 - 10 - 8;   6 - 5 - 10 - (8)

16. 7 - 3 - 9 - 4;   7 - 3 - 9 - (4)

17. 17 - 13 - 8 - 14;   17 - 13 - 8 - (14)

18. 12 - 16 - 11 - 18;   12 - 16 - 11 - (18)

19. 9 - 17 - 20 - 12;   9 - 17 - 20 - (12)

20. 19 - 11 - 8 - 12;   19 - 11 - 8 - (12)

21. 10 - 18 - 16 - 15;   10 - 18 - 16 - (15)

22. 16 - 14 - 18 - 11;   16 - 14 - 18 - (11)

23. 99 - 83 - 91 - 72;   99 - 83 - 91 - (72)

24. 81 - 64 - 33 - 23;   81 - 64 - 33 - (23)

25. 71 - 18 - 96 - 98;   71 - 18 - 96 - (98)

26. 85 - 91 - 101 - 46;   85 - 91 - 101 - (46)

27. 21 - 74 - 183 - 52;   21 - 74 - 183 - (52)

28. 42 - 68 - 66 - 81;   42 - 68 - 66 - (81)

29. 56 - 35 - 27 - 77;   56 - 35 - 27 - (77)

30. 33 - 46 - 58 - 43;   33 - 46 - 58 - (43)

IV. Memory of two items in a three-unit sequence

The items in section II may be used with the last *two* digits of the sequence omitted.

Examples: 1.   3 - 5 - 1;   3 - (5) - (1)

2.   17 - 13 - 8;   17 - (13) - (8)

V. Memory of two items in a four-unit sequence

The items in section III may be used with the last *two* digits of the sequence omitted.

Examples: 1.   7 - 3 - 9 - 4;   7 - 3 - (9) - (4)

          2.   56 - 46 - 58 - 43;   56 - 46 - (58) - (43)

VI. Memory of three items in a four-unit sequence

The items in section III may be used with the last *three* digits of the sequence omitted.

Examples: 1.   8 - 3 - 7 - 9;   8 - (3) - (7) - (9)

          2.   71 - 18 - 96 - 89;   71 - (18) - (96) - (89)

VII. Memory of four items in a four-unit sequence

The items in section III may be used with the student repeating all four digits in the sequence.

Examples: 1.   85 - 91 - 101 - 46;   (85) - (91) - (101) - (46)

          2.   9 - 4 - 1 - 3;   (9) - (4) - (1) - (3)

I.E.P. Goal: When presented aloud with digits in progressively longer patterns, the client will, upon hearing part of the pattern repeated, insert the missing number or numbers with 90% or greater accuracy.

Auditory Memory
Task B: Recognition Memory for Words in a Pattern

Listen to the patterns of words I say. I will repeat part of the words. You say the part I don't say.

I. Memory of one item in a two-unit sequence

1. car - bird; car - (bird)

2. truck - plane; truck - (plane)

3. book - pad; book - (pad)

4. chair - wing; chair - (wing)

5. horse - bath; horse - (bath)

6. foot - bike; foot - (bike)

7. fix - time; fix - (time)

8. light - rug; light - (rug)

9. glass - hair; glass - (hair)

10. tray - cup; tray - (cup)

11. bake - top; bake - (top)

12. shoe - night; shoe - (night)

13. hot - month; hot - (month)

14. door - pear; door - (pear)

15. wood - cup; wood - (cup)

16. pen - step; pen - (step)

17. lock - ear; lock - (ear)

18. air - dot; air - (dot)

19. bed - leaf; bed - (leaf)

20. eye - pan; eye - (pan)

21. floor - clip; floor - (clip)

22. pants - bath; pants - (bath)

23. book - tree; book - (tree)

24. lamp - gem; lamp - (gem)

25. toe - chalk; toe - (chalk)

26. silk - watch; silk - (watch)

27. mark - ring; mark - (ring)

28. desk - pick; desk - (pick)

29. knot - girl; knot - (girl)

30. bloom - nail; bloom - (nail)

II. Memory of one item in a three-unit sequence

1. box - shoe - soap; box - shoe - (soap)

2. knife - hat - book; knife - hat - (book)

3. bus - tag - door; bus - tag - (door)

4. shirt - light - nail; shirt - light - (nail)

5. glass - hair - cup; glass - hair - (cup)

6. plant - bed - pen; plant - bed - (pen)

7. sled - soap - doll; sled - soap - (doll)

8. beef - jacks - game; beef - jacks - (game)

9. dog - sand - bean; dog - sand - (bean)

10. rose - board - beets; rose - board - (beets)

11. vase - plane - pill; vase - plane - (pill)

12. horse - slide - bear; horse - slide - (bear)

13. spade - log - pad; spade - log - (pad)

14. ball - sit - wheel; ball - sit - (wheel)

15. stand - crib - gown; stand - crib - (gown)

16. comb - bow - blue; comb - bow - (blue)

17. owl - train - box; owl - train - (box)

18. stove - seed - ant; stove - seed - (ant)

19. hoe - tie - paint; hoe - tie - (paint)

20. pail - fork - bell; pail - fork - (bell)

21. jet - eye - whale; jet - eye - (whale)

22. jam - scale - hole; jam - scale - (hole)

23. skate - oil - tug; skate - oil - (tug)

24. moth - bead - shop; moth - bead - (shop)

25. pan - salt - lake; pan - salt - (lake)

26. brick - tape - gas; brick - tape - (gas)

27. nut - fire - drum; nut - fire - (drum)

28. frog - key - pond; frog - key - (pond)

29. pie - spool - bag; pie - spool - (bag)

30. jar - raft - cake; jar - raft - (cake)

III. Memory of one item in a four-unit sequence

1. foot - race - peach - silk; foot - race - peach - (silk)

2. land - cat - beard - ghost; land - cat - beard - (ghost)

3. back - desk - spoon - bin; back - desk - spoon - (bin)

4. fish - tack - pot - shelf; fish - tack - pot - (shelf)

5. dress - bell - dust - soap; dress - bell - dust - (soap)

6. lamp - flag - broom - fort; lamp - flag - broom - (fort)

7. bed - ink - can - tray; bed - ink - can - (tray)

8. plant - clay - tea - nurse; plant - clay - tea - (nurse)

9. bone - paste - stool - dance; bone - paste - stool - (dance)

10. heart - milk - queen - dump; heart - milk - queen - (dump)

11. ice - chalk - egg - dirt; ice - chalk - egg - (dirt)

12. sand - clock - shell - bull; sand - clock - shell - (bull)

13. tin - wall - dig - ox; tin - wall - dig - (ox)

14. ball - sit - wheel - coach; ball - sit - wheel - (coach)

15. pin - squash - cone - star; pine - squash - cone - (star)

16. ant - net - clown - dog; ant - net - clown - (dog)

17. saw - cage - car - boot; saw - cage - car - (boot)

18. tent - pole - horn - coal; tent - pole - horn - (coal)

19. rail - felt - shell - seed; rail - felt - shell - (seed)

20. spike - fish - house - pond; spike - fish - house - (pond)

21. gate - beach - string - fly; gate - beach - string - (fly)

22. barn - oar - drop - dock; barn - oar - drop - (dock)

23. nest - skate - rain - lamb; nest - skate - rain - (lamb)

24. switch - sand - cloud - kite; switch - sand - cloud - (kite)

25. stork - sun - brush - glue; stork - sun - brush - (glue)

26. stairs - mud - mop - rock; stairs - mud - mop - (rock)

27. swan - wire - cave - stone; swan - wire - cave - (stone)

28. coat - print - rink - smoke; coat - print - rink - (smoke)

29. stalk - boot - wrench - rake; stalk - boot - wrench - (rake)

30. suds - chest - sheet - toy; suds - chest - sheet - (toy)

IV. Memory of two items in three- and four-unit sequences
The items in sections II and III may be used with the last *two* words of the sequence omitted.

Examples: 1. glass - hair - cup; glass - (hair) - (cup)

2. barn - oar - drop - dock; barn - oar - (drop) - (dock)

V. Memory of three items in a four-unit sequence
The items in section III may be used with the last *three* words of the sequence omitted.

Examples: 1. rose - board - bee - vase; rose - (board) - (bee) - (vase)

2. suds - chest - sheet - toy; suds - (chest) - (sheet) - (toy)

VI. Memory of four items in a four-unit sequence
The items in section III may be used with all *four* words in the sequence to be repeated by the student.

Examples: 1. swan - wire - cave - stone; (swan) - (wire) - (cave) - (stone)

2. stairs - mud - mop - rock; (stairs) - (mud) - (mop) - (rock)

I.E.P. Goal: The client will repeat the missing word or words in a progressively longer pattern presented aloud with 90% or greater accuracy.

Note: The exercises in this section (VI) are the same task as the exercises in the sections for Sequential Memory for Related and Unrelated Words. Please refer to these tasks later in this chapter for additional exercises.

Auditory Memory
Task C: Recognition Memory for Facts in a Sentence

Note: This section incorporates the pre-requisite skill of answering *Wh*-Questions. Please refer to Chapter 3 in HELP, Volume II for exercises pertaining to this skill area.

Listen to each sentence I read. Then, answer the question I ask you about what I read.

1. I ate a roast beef sandwich for lunch.
What did I eat?   (roast beef sandwich)

2. The old man waved a stick at me.
What did the old man wave?   (a stick)

3. The lamp fell over during the wind storm.
When did the lamp fall?   (during the wind storm)

4. The tumble-down house had no door and the windows had locks but no glass.
   What did the windows have?   (locks)

5. The cows are in the pasture, where there is a lot of grass.
   Where are the cows?   (in the pasture)

6. Sherry drank her chocolate shake and ate a piece of strawberry pie.
   What flavor was her shake?   (chocolate)

7. The fifty-foot building was lost amid the skyscrapers.
   How tall was the building?   (fifty feet)

8. The floor has a gold rug and the window has green curtains.
   What color is the rug?   (gold)

9. The laundry was to be delivered to the rear of the store.
   What was to be delivered?   (laundry)

10. Mrs. Smith is a gracious hostess.
    Who is the hostess?   (Mrs. Smith)

11. Mr. Johnson was a super history teacher this year.
    What did he teach?   (history)
    What was his name?   (Mr. Johnson)

12. Yesterday, Tom fell over a rock and hurt his knee.
    What did Tom fall over?   (a rock)
    What did Tom hurt?   (his knee)

13. On Monday, we went to the store and bought some eggs.
    What day did we go to the store?   (on Monday)
    What did we buy?   (eggs)

14. Mike put the blue car in the garage and then went to a friend's house.
    What did Mike put in the garage?   (a blue car)
    Where did Mike go?   (to a friend's house)

15. The cat ate the yellow canary.
    What kind of bird did he eat?   (canary)
    What color was the bird?   (yellow)

16. Uncle Bill fell down the stairs and broke his leg and sprained his hand.
    What did he sprain?   (hand)
    Who fell?   (Uncle Bill)

17. The water pipes froze and broke last night.
    Which pipes froze?   (the water pipes)
    When did it happen?   (last night)

18. The birthday gifts made the little girl happy.
    Who was happy?   (the little girl)
    What was given?   (birthday gifts)

19. The old man lived in a gray shack.
    Where did he live?   (in a shack)
    What color was the shack?   (gray)

20. The house on Broad Street is a mansion.
    Where is the house?   (on Broad Street)
    What kind of house is it?   (a mansion)

21. Dad gave Mary a ten-dollar bill.
    Who received the money?   (Mary)
    Who gave the money?   (Dad)
    How much money did Mary receive?   ($10)

22. John has enough money to buy the new automobile.
    What is John going to buy?   (an automobile)
    What does he have enough of?   (money)
    Who is buying the car?   (John)

23. The secret of the old house was told by old man George every Halloween.
    What was the secret about?   (the old house)
    Who told the story?   (old man; George)
    When did he tell the secret?   (on Halloween)

24. The sweet woman who lives in the house on the corner gave the youngsters a slice of cake.
    What did the youngsters receive?   (a slice of cake)
    Who gave it to them?   (the woman)
    Where does the woman live?   (in the house on the corner)

25. The Johnson family takes their boat to the lake every weekend.
    Where does the family go?   (to the lake)
    When do they go?   (on the weekend)
    What do they take with them?   (their boat)
    What is the name of the family?   (Johnson)

Note: The following exercises involve the same basic memory skill as above. In addition, these exercises also tap categorical knowledge. (Refer to Chapter 2: Categorization in HELP, Volume II.)

1. A little boy was wearing a red jacket.
   What color did I say?   (red)

2. A leopard is a fast animal with many spots.
   What animal did I say?   (leopard)

3. On Thursday, I go to my Boy Scout meeting.
   What day did I say?   (Thursday)

4. My dog, Fred, likes to swim in the lake.
   What name did I say?   (Fred)

5. My school isn't very far from here.
   What place did I say?   (school)

6. My dad's car is blue with silver trim.
   What transportation did I say?   (car)

7. My brother is sixteen years old.
   What number did I say?   (16)

8. A Labrador is a kind pet.
   What kind of animal did I say?   (Labrador or dog)

9. The bed was burned during the fire.
   What furniture did I say?   (bed)

10. The mail carrier brought us a package today.
    What person did I say? (mail carrier)

11. The balloon blew away in the breeze.
    What toy did I say?   (balloon)

12. The silver melted in the extreme heat.
    What metal did I say?   (silver)

13. Mary ate a piece of chocolate cake after dinner.
    What dessert did I say?   (chocolate cake)

14. The old man is a carpenter.
    What occupation did I say?   (carpenter)

15. Michael and Terry love to play baseball.
    What sport did I say?   (baseball)

16. The three women lived in a mansion.
    What house did I say?   (mansion)

17. The green beans and bacon were delicious.
    What vegetable did I say?   (green beans)

18. The Chevrolet broke down at the intersection.
    What car did I say?   (Chevrolet)

19. The sofa was damaged by the move.
    What furniture did I say?   (sofa)

20. The licorice was black and chewy.
    What candy did I say?   (licorice)

I.E.P. Goal: When presented aloud with a sentence, the client will respond appropriately to one or more questions regarding the content of the sentence with 90% or greater accuracy.

Task D: Sequential Memory for Related Words

Listen to the words I say.   Repeat the words in the same order I said them.

I.   Memory of three-unit sequences

1. chair - bed - desk
2. horn - drum - bell
3. brown - orange - purple
4. pail - mop - broom
5. bag - box - jar
6. teeth - ear - nose
7. seed - plant - hoe
8. bus - boat - plane
9. shoe - dress - slip
10. log - axe - saw
11. pan - pot - stove
12. glass - cup - mug
13. dog - cat - cow
14. clock - watch - time
15. peach - pear - orange
16. heart - bone - teeth
17. dance - sit - run
18. tent - pole - camp
19. skate - ice - snow
20. suds - soap - wash
21. floor - wall - door
22. girl - boy - man
23. month - day - year
24. air - wind - breeze
25. clip - glue - tape
26. beets - beans - corn
27. pork - hog - pig
28. blue - white - pink
29. fork - spoon - knife
30. car - train - boat

II.   Memory of four-unit sequences

1. stove - bake - pie - cake
2. hot - burn - fire - coal
3. desk - pen - write - learn
4. pants - shirt - sock - shoe
5. night - dark - sleep - moon
6. book - chalk - school - pen
7. king - prince - queen - knight
8. chain - rope - gate - lock
9. oak - tree - root - leaf
10. tea - milk - Coke - shake
11. drum - kite - ball - rope
12. wife - church - ring - white
13. zip - snap - clip - hook
14. glove - hat - boot - coat

137

15. swing - slide - sand - toys
16. toast - bread - wheat - flour
17. lamp - light - sun - moon
18. rail - train - wheels - cars
19. song - note - play - tune
20. fly - bug - ant - wasp
21. sick - ache - ill - weak
22. hoe - seed - plant - food

23. whale - fish - shark - eel
24. spool - sew - thread - pin
25. jar - box - cage - bowl
26. rose - bud - bush - bloom
27. beef - pork - ham - fish
28. back - front - side - top
29. comb - brush - hair - wash
30. jet - plane - wing - fly

III. Memory of five-unit sequences

1. pants - shirt - shoe - hat - belt
2. fork - knife - spoon - plate - glass
3. warm - cold - hot - fire - ice
4. eggs - toast - milk - juice - jam
5. hall - stairs - wall - floor - door
6. skate - rope - ball - jacks - slide
7. toss - throw - roll - bounce - catch
8. saw - file - drill - wrench - bolt
9. hen - chick - pig - goat - sheep
10. cow - hay - grass - fence - farm
11. plane - blimp - kite - jet - wing
12. game - blocks - truck - bike - doll
13. corn - beans - peas - squash - beets
14. boat - barge - ship - raft - float
15. blouse - suit - cap - tie - gloves

16. paint - brush - ink - pen - smock
17. one - six - five - two - four
18. car - bus - truck - train - plane
19. pond - bay - lake - beach - stream
20. chalk - paste - desk - school - book
21. dough - egg - milk - flour - salt
22. mop - broom - sponge - dust - dirt
23. fort - school - church - store - house
24. wash - soap - tub - sink - bath
25. sit - stand - run - walk - jump
26. in - out - on - off - up
27. thin - tall - short - long - fat
28. hawk - owl - crane - stork - goose
29. clam - crab - shark - eel - shrimp
30. seeds - rake - hoe - hose - plant

I.E.P. Goal: When presented aloud with related, monosyllabic words in progressively longer sequences, the client will repeat the words in the same order with 90% or greater accuracy.

Task E: Sequential Memory for Unrelated Words

Listen to the words I say.   Repeat the words in the same order I said them.

I. Memory of three-unit sequences

1. fall - boy - good
2. sing - bag - long
3. oak - send - cup
4. rub - fire - man
5. lunch - hop - gas
6. dark - eat - dig
7. zip - king - phone
8. cake - shirt - gum
9. mat - oat - door
10. tie - jail - book
11. desk - like - ring
12. chain - dog - say
13. ace - floor - bed
14. kiss - bear - group
15. box - rope - wet

16. car - hole - feet
17. bird - moth - wheel
18. truck - board - car
19. light - beds - horn
20. pen - glass - cage
21. car - hat - bar
22. lamp - hair - base
23. silk - owl - chalk
24. mark - train - tin
25. girl - salt - paste
26. pie - key - ghost
27. knot - pond - sheet
28. frog - bus - wrench
29. beef - tag - swan
30. doll - wake - tray

II. Memory of four-unit sequences

1. bend - land - with - fish
2. write - choose - green - cone
3. back - lung - judge - fire
4. sick - fig - bone - door
5. bike - limp - hat - slab
6. mouth - bent - trip - worth
7. loud - star - rise - silk

8. fog - went - glass - coat
9. lock - toast - pail - sir
10. back - lose - zoo - skirt
11. pen - web - clock - tree
12. rock - ball - rug - light
13. pot - car - meat - block
14. grain - hose - lamp - boot

15. ring - wait - send - prince

16. mud - chest - shell - dock

17. ice - chalk - flag - sit

18. back - cage - hole - pen

19. sand - tent - wall - heart

20. race - log - rose - pitch

21. pass - salt - doll - out

22. teeth - stop - bike - pear

23. girl - air - rug - knot

24. pig - be - sit - door

25. book - glue - broom - ace

26. desk - soap - egg - blue

27. night - time - pie - reel

28. king - ink - roast - hoe

29. meal - pail - red - food

30. ash - fig - parts - cake

III. Memory of five-unit sequences

1. wake - group - stain - tea - seal

2. meal - go - way - bake - fleet

3. rail - boat - game - wall - torn

4. rake - bought - base - late - rain

5. hose - price - face - bike - wet

6. beam - steep - pale - slate - hire

7. heat - please - led - chart - will

8. cane - maid - lip - rack - sun

9. cake - black - wing - ban - soap

10. coat - shag - trap - chick - skirt

11. part - crush - drop - fly - box

12. pace - drug - eye - ash - end

13. sand - boat - fly - oak - girl

14. bad - frog - tag - tack - mat

15. cup - man - jail - kiss - cat

16. chart - dump - in - cot - call

17. pig - lamp - pen - ask - ape

18. seen - ice - old - time - day

19. sent - done - toad - kite - him

20. team - no - snip - lead - bay

21. hide - spell - pact - ray - ship

22. life - jump - if - pet - zoo

23. gem - nail - star - poke - by

24. knot - log - sat - rink - swan

25. horse - steak - beard - drop - bar

26. coach - squash - ink - bacon - gate

27. pin - raft - milk - spring - swan

28. rose - shell - chalk - sing - box

29. pail - spot - cage - bail - beans

30. shop - shelf - hour - tray - wash

I.E.P. Goal: When presented aloud with unrelated, monosyllabic words in progressively longer sequences, the client will repeat the words in the same order with 90% or greater accuracy.

Task F: Sequential Memory for Digits

Listen to the numbers I say.   Repeat the numbers in the same order I said them.

I. Memory of three-unit sequences

1.	6 - 1 - 7		16.	14 - 23 - 9
2.	3 - 8 - 6		17.	91 - 27 - 88
3.	8 - 5 - 7		18.	121 - 17 - 1
4.	7 - 4 - 1		19.	111 - 41 - 44
5.	3 - 9 - 4		20.	64 - 12 - 22
6.	8 - 1 - 7		21.	183 - 74 - 16
7.	7 - 6 - 2		22.	66 - 99 - 32
8.	3 - 4 - 4		23.	58 - 33 - 19
9.	10 - 7 - 6		24.	10 - 9 - 7
10.	1 - 4 - 3		25.	85 - 43 - 1
11.	18 - 10 - 13		26.	83 - 63 - 101
12.	6 - 3 - 8		27.	58 - 28 - 3
13.	10 - 5 - 6		28.	11 - 17 - 52
14.	3 - 7 - 5		29.	20 - 4 - 37
15.	9 - 2 - 4		30.	8 - 68 - 20

II. Memory of four-unit sequences

1.	5 - 2 - 1 - 7		8.	3 - 5 - 1 - 7
2.	8 - 3 - 9 - 4		9.	9 - 8 - 4 - 18
3.	2 - 10 - 4 - 6		10.	7 - 6 - 8 - 1
4.	1 - 4 - 3 - 2		11.	11 - 4 - 13 - 2
5.	8 - 4 - 7 - 2		12.	9 - 5 - 7 - 1
6.	6 - 1 - 10 - 3		13.	13 - 19 - 3 - 20
7.	4 - 7 - 9 - 2		14.	16 - 1 - 14 - 8

15.	17 - 4 - 9 - 3	23.	85 - 16 - 103 - 43
16.	10 - 52 - 7 - 16	24.	72 - 42 - 11 - 38
17.	8 - 1 - 17 - 80	25.	53 - 96 - 70 - 64
18.	17 - 6 - 9 - 25	26.	66 - 23 - 152 - 78
19.	49 - 4 - 27 - 30	27.	47 - 17 - 171 - 25
20.	21 - 41 - 77 - 36	28.	99 - 4 - 19 - 32
21.	23 - 41 - 77 - 36	29.	82 - 33 - 27 - 43
22.	37 - 18 - 100 - 5	30.	19 - 78 - 46 - 91

III. Memory of five-unit sequences

1.	7 - 8 - 1 - 9 - 3	16.	11 - 6 - 9 - 10 - 7
2.	1 - 5 - 6 - 8 - 7	17.	30 - 18 - 5 - 1 - 16
3.	3 - 4 - 9 - 1 - 2	18.	22 - 5 - 18 - 20 - 9
4.	5 - 7 - 8 - 4 - 9	19.	18 - 22 - 14 - 5 - 37
5.	2 - 9 - 3 - 7 - 1	20.	16 - 7 - 31 - 6 - 50
6.	9 - 1 - 0 - 5 - 6	21.	51 - 3 - 10 - 5 - 8
7.	4 - 10 - 8 - 6 - 3	22.	36 - 5 - 17 - 1 - 61
8.	6 - 6 - 1 - 7 - 8	23.	19 - 9 - 44 - 10 - 5
9.	8 - 5 - 7 - 2 - 6	24.	37 - 14 - 31 - 70 - 18
10.	10 - 21 - 6 - 7 - 8	25.	94 - 76 - 16 - 21 - 4
11.	13 - 8 - 7 - 1 - 4	26.	83 - 52 - 9 - 16 - 10
12.	12 - 11 - 5 - 0 - 10	27.	75 - 104 - 88 - 4 - 100
13.	19 - 5 - 2 - 9 - 3	28.	46 - 87 - 62 - 7 - 11
14.	4 - 5 - 2 - 9 - 3	29.	32 - 2 - 6 - 100 - 62
15.	14 - 1 - 3 - 10 - 5	30.	61 - 111 - 7 - 9 - 89

I.E.P. Goal: When presented aloud with digits in progressively longer sequences, the client will repeat the digits in the same order with 90% or greater accuracy.

Task G: Sequential Memory for Following Directions

I.   Sequential Memory for Single-Stage Commands with Concrete Objects

I'm going to tell you to do some things with these objects.   Listen carefully, and do just what I tell you to do.

Suggested objects: ball, paper, cup, soap, block, shoe, book, key, marble, pencil, bell, box, hat, etc.

1. Pick up the ball.
2. Ring the bell.
3. Put the soap under the table.
4. Put the key in the box.
5. Put the spoon on the paper.
6. Pick up the shoe.
7. Open the book.
8. Hold the key.
9. Put the marble in the cup.
10. Rip the paper.
11. Bounce the ball.
12. Put on the hat.
13. Put the block on the table.
14. Write with the pencil.
15. Open the box.
16. Put the block next to the box.
17. Read the book.
18. Open the door.
19. Give the pencil to me.
20. Put the key in your pocket.

I.E.P. Goal: The client will follow single-stage commands presented aloud, using concrete objects, with 90% or greater accuracy.

II.   Sequential Memory for Single-Stage Commands with Body Movements.

I'm going to tell you to do some things.   Listen carefully, and do just what I tell you to do.

1. Put your hand on your head.
2. Sit down.
3. Walk to the door.
4. Open the door.
5. Raise your hand.
6. Hop up and down.
7. Close your eyes.
8. Turn around.
9. Clap your hands twice.
10. Wave good-bye.
11. Put your elbow on your knee.
12. Cross your legs.
13. Put your head down on the table.
14. Cover your eyes with your hands.

15.	Stand on one foot.	18.	Snap your fingers once.
16.	Kneel on the floor.	19.	Touch your back.
17.	Wiggle your nose.	20.	Touch your toes.

I.E.P. Goal: The client will follow single-stage commands presented aloud, pertaining to body movements, with 90% or greater accuracy.

III. Sequential Memory for Two- and Three-Stage Commands

I'm going to tell you to do some things. Listen carefully, and do just what I tell you to do.

Suggested objects: book, paper, box, key, hat, soap, pencil, chalk, chalkboard

1. Clap your hands; pick up the book.

2. Stand up; touch your hair.

3. Write on the paper; put your hand on your head.

4. Say your name; close your eyes.

5. Put the key next to the box; walk to me.

6. Open the door; say "hello."

7. Sit down; close your eyes.

8. Stand up; hop three times.

9. Rip the paper; throw it away.

10. Put on your hat; turn around twice.

11. Pick up the soap; hold it above your head.

12. Put your right hand behind your back; put your left hand in your pocket.

13. Give the pencil to me; touch your nose.

14. Walk to the window; turn around.

15. Place the key in your pocket; hum aloud.

16. Put your hands in your lap; nod your head.

17. Write your name in the air; smile.

18. Shake your head "no" two times; raise your hand.

19. Put your hand on your head; slap your knee.

20. Stand up; turn off the light.

21. Say "good-bye;" walk to the door.

22. Turn on the light; clap your hands.

23. Pick up your coat; turn around twice.

24. Walk to the chalkboard; draw a circle on it.

25. Open your mouth; stick out your tongue.

26. Shut your eyes; say your name.

27. Stand up; push in your chair.

28. Touch the desk; put your hand under the table.

29. Wave at the door; put both hands on your head.

30. Pretend to drink from a glass; wipe your mouth.

The directions from section I, II, and III may be used in sequences of three commands to complete criterion for this section.

I.E.P. Goal: *The client will follow two- and three-stage commands presented aloud with 90% or greater accuracy.*

IV. Sequential Memory for Four-Stage Commands

The goal and directions from sections I, II and III may be used in sequences of four commands to complete criterion for this section.

Auditory Memory
Task H: Memory for Sentences of 3- to 6-Word Length

Listen to each sentence I say. Then, you say the sentence exactly the same way.

1. Open the door.

2. Please don't go.

3. I like to eat raisins.

4. Please answer the telephone.

5. Call me later tonight.

6. She walked up the steps.

7. The bag was full of trash.

8. Sometimes even doctors get sick.

9. Never cross the street without looking.

10. Snowflakes have eight sides.

11. Don't call unless you're coming.

12. March 17th is St. Patrick's Day.

13. I asked her to go.

14. Chairs are for sitting.

15. Animals live in the zoo.

16. Glasses can break if dropped.

17. Cakes and pies are my favorites.

18. Drink all of your milk.

19. Put out the light.

20. Raise your hand before you speak.

21. Books are fun to read.

22. I would like a bicycle.

23. Potato chips taste too salty.

24. Here he comes down the street.

25. The boy fell down the steps.

26. He bought a little car.

27. I don't know what you're saying.

28. I will go get some money.

29. I can't help it.

30. Kids love the circus animals.

31. The farmer raked the garden.

32. Lightning and thunder scare me.

33. The houseboat had ten rooms.

34. The bluefish weighed eleven pounds.

35. Railroad stations are my favorite places.

36. The circus horse does many tricks.

37. I know my alphabet and numbers.

38. I make bread with my mother.

39. Santa Claus visits at Christmas.

40. Black cats bring bad luck.

41. Ice cream and cake taste good together.

42. Fireworks are seen on July 4th.

43. The fire hydrant broke yesterday.

44. The police car lost control.

45. The statue broke in the square.

46. Pastels are beautiful colors to use.

47. I need a pad of paper.

48. A sea lion is unusual.

49. The gorilla escaped from his cage.

50. The turkey tasted good on Thanksgiving.

I.E.P. Goal: the client will repeat verbatim a three- to six-word sentence presented aloud with 90% or greater accuracy.

Auditory Memory
Task I: Memory for Sentences of 6- to 10-Word Length

Listen to each sentence I say.   Then, you say the sentence exactly the same way.

1. Mary and Jane went to school on Monday.

2. Playing hopscotch is a lot of fun.

3. You have to work hard in school to do well.

4. The football popped when it hit the rake.

5. I can't seem to find the key to the door.

6. She can't come over to play right now.

7. If you tell me what to do, I will go.

8. The oven is full of pies, cakes and cookies.

9. Never be out of your house late at night.

10. The book was ripped and worn from use.

11. Margaret told me how the movie was going to end.

12. The telephone fell off the wall this morning.

13. I hope you can help the little boy get home.

14. Sometimes people aren't very nice to one another.

15. Open the drawer and put the money in there.

16. I wouldn't want to go home by myself.

17. Don't jump or you might break your leg.

18. Be careful when you are near a skunk.

19. Sarah can't wait until the party next week.

20. The Easter Bunny will leave you good things to eat.

21. Don't give up if you lose the first time.

22. Wash your face and hands before dinner.

23. The tree was struck by lightning during the storm.

24. Please be careful not to break the window.

25. Coin collecting is a very expensive but interesting hobby.

26. Tomorrow night, there will be fireworks at the park.

27. I can never tell how many we use in a day.

28. Sometimes people don't mean what they say in haste.

29. The furniture was delivered before the store could call.

30. If you would like to go with me, you may.

31. The garbage truck rolled away when the brakes failed.

32. The little boy hit a baseball through the neighbor's window.

33. The paper carrier collected an extra fifty dollars in tips.

34. Digital watches have taken over the watch industry.

35. Many children fill their summers with swimming, camp and baseball.

36. Bingo is a game enjoyed by young and old alike.

37. The grocer bought too many eggs and not enough lettuce.

38. Automobiles require constant maintenance and tender loving care.

39. Contact lenses have become extremely popular with all ages.

40. The average life span for Americans is seventy years.

41. Put the sweater in the cedar chest beside the blankets.

42. Eric asked his father if the charcoal was ready.

43. Hiking, swimming and camping are popular summer activities.

44. Knives are sold in the housewares department in the basement.

45. Down-filled quilts are both warm and lightweight.

46. Expensive items should be insured before mailing.

47. The crash of the falling tree echoed throughout the forest.

48. Our flight to Toronto was twenty minutes late upon departure.

49. Museums preserve our culture and history for all to enjoy.

50. Hang-gliding is becoming a very popular sport in many areas.

I.E.P. Goal: The client will repeat verbatim a six- to ten-word sentence presented aloud with 90% or greater accuracy.

Auditory Memory
Task J: Memory for Paragraphs - Two-Sentence Length

Listen carefully to what I read.   Then, tell me the important information in what I read.   Tell me the information in the order I read it.

1. Sue and Ellen went to the store today.   They only had five cents, so they bought two pieces of bubble gum.

2. Jack couldn't find his shirt where he had left it.   He went downstairs to ask his mom and found his dog sleeping on it.

3. Two men were walking down the street and noticed a wallet on the street.   They picked it up and found a thousand dollars in it.

4. To make bread, you need more than just a pan and an oven. You also need some flour, yeast and salt, to name a few things.

5. Michael couldn't believe his ears. He had been chosen to ride his pony in the Labor Day parade.

6. Seven inches of snow fell on the ground last night. We dug out the car and then made a snowman.

7. The farmer, who lives north of town, was lost in the big city. He finally asked a police officer to help him on his way.

8. Mother arranged the flowers in a vase. She put them in the bedroom so she could see them as she sewed.

9. The big store across the street is having a closing sale. You will have to hurry to save some money on pants and shirts.

10. The wolves came out of the forest in the moonlight. They were tired and wet, having run ten miles in the snow.

I.E.P. Goal: The client will recall in sequence significant facts in a two-sentence paragraph presented aloud with 90% or greater accuracy.

Auditory Memory
Task K: Memory for Paragraphs - Three-Sentence Length

Listen carefully to what I read. Then, tell me the important information in what I read. Tell me the information in the order I read it.

1. The ice cream truck came down the road. All the children ran to ask their mothers for some money. Then they all bought chocolate ice cream.

2. One day a little boy went to a pet store. There he saw a puppy, three kittens, and a monkey. He liked the monkey best of all.

3. The little boy went to his friend's house to watch TV. They watched "Tarzan" and "Superman." Then they both fell asleep on the floor.

4. Jenny was having a birthday party. She was going to be five years old. Her mother baked her a cake and bought her some chocolate-vanilla-strawberry ice cream.

5. His mother asked Tommy what he wanted for Christmas. "A big red fire truck," he said. "And a blue and white police car to help with the fires."

6. When asked what he liked most about school, George replied, "I like break time and gym class. I also like geography. But most of all, I like school when the bell rings and we can go home."

7. Doug and his girlfriend went to the lake on Sunday. They went swimming and sailing until noon. They enjoyed a picnic lunch of apples, sandwiches, lemonade and cookies.

8. It always smells good right before it rains.   The air gets cool and it becomes windy. Then the rain begins suddenly, with big drops pelting down.

9. The carnival comes to our town each June.   Since our town is very small and there is not much to do here, people look forward to the carnival for months.   When it arrives, you can see everyone you know walking around the grounds.

10. Mr. Anderson, a lawyer, said that it was the toughest case he had ever taken.   The evidence had been destroyed and there were no witnesses to be found.   He certainly had his work cut out for him.

I.E.P. Goal: The client will recall in sequence significant facts in a three-sentence paragraph presented aloud with 90% or greater accuracy.

Auditory Memory
Task L: Memory for Paragraphs of Four or More Sentences

Listen carefully to what I read.   Then, tell me the important information in what I read.   Tell me the information in the order I read it.

1. Basketball is a team sport.   It involves five players, a ball and a hoop or a basket. By bouncing or passing the ball, a team may score two points by getting the ball in the other team's basket.   The team with the most points at the end of thirty minutes wins.

2. After dinner, most people enjoy eating dessert.   Desserts such as fruit, pies and cakes are popular with adults and children alike.   Children especially like cookies.   Ice cream is a favorite of all in the summertime.

3. If you can catch a firefly, you might be able to make a cage for it.   Take a clean, dry jar, placing some greenery in the bottom.   Attach a wire screen over the jar opening with a rubber band or tight string.   This allows air to flow in and out of the jar for the insect.

4. As we were driving down Orange Avenue, we heard the scream of a police siren.   Dad pulled the car over to the side of the road as the police car approached us from behind.   It sped past us and turned the corner sharply.   The following day, we read of a bank hold-up in the newspaper.

5. Large libraries keep microfilm copies of newspapers in order to conserve space. Smaller libraries usually discard back issues.   Most newspaper offices have a morgue, which is where copies of all back issues are kept.   These sources are open to the public to be used in research.

6. Before a potter molds clay, the clay must be worked thoroughly to remove all air bubbles.   This process is known as wedging the clay.   The next step is to center the clay on the wheel and pull up the sides of the pot.   Experienced potters make this process look very easy, when in fact it requires much skill.

7. Many spectators believe women's lacrosse is a dangerous sport. To the contrary, unlike men's lacrosse, no physical contact between the players is allowed and rough use of the stick is forbidden. Women's lacrosse is a more graceful sport requiring skill, endurance and coordination.

8. In April, 1912, one of the world's greatest ocean liners, the *Titanic*, sank. Everyone, including the company which built her, believed the *Titanic* was unsinkable. On her maiden voyage she ran into icebergs. They ripped a hole in her bow, causing her to sink.

9. The best known of all prehistoric men is the Neanderthal man. They lived during the period of the last ice age. Their skulls jutted out in the back and their foreheads were low. They made a variety of weapons, axes and tools.

10. Pavlov was a psychologist known for his research with digestive glands. While experimenting, he found that the salivation of dogs could be stimulated by learning. He conditioned the dog to the sound of a ringing bell. After the dog was conditioned, it would begin to salivate when it heard the bell.

I.E.P. Goal: The client will recall in sequence significant facts in a paragraph of four sentences or more presented aloud with 90% or greater accuracy.

Note: If the student has difficulty recalling the significant facts in the paragraphs presented above, leading questions may be asked in order to facilitate recall. Examples of appropriate questions for paragraph 3 are as follows:

  1. What type of insect is this story about?
  2. Do you use a wet or dry jar for the insect?
  3. Should you put a lid on the jar? Why not?

Additional paragraphs from textbooks or library books may be used in therapy to provide further material for practicing memory for paragraphs.

Auditory Memory: General Activities

1. To build memory for sequence, use words and numbers printed on index cards.   Use the following order of activities with either set of cards:

    Using two cards, place them face up on the table and have the student point to the cards in sequence from left to right, naming each as he does so.

    Turn one of the cards over and point to the cards once again in left to right sequence, naming each as it is pointed to; the student must remember the item on the card which has been turned face down.

    Turn both cards face down, once again pointing to each in left to right sequence and naming each card as it is pointed to.   The student must remember both cards; the position of the cards on the table will serve as a cue.   Name the cards without pointing to them and then take up the cards and name them once again.   Continue this activity with longer sequences of cards.

    As the student acquires proficiency, steps of this process may be eliminated.   For example, the student may be able to name the cards when all have been turned face down after seeing the faces of the cards only one time.

2. Give the child a password when he enters the room.   Ask for recall of this word throughout the session.   Use the word as a pass for leaving the room at the end of the session.   Progress to phrases and sentences of increasing length and difficulty.

3. Use comic strips pasted on index cards to sequence a short story.   Lay the cards on the table in sequence as the student watches and use a brief sentence to tell what is happening in each frame.   Then take up the cards and mix the order.   Give them to the student and instruct the student to place the cards on the table in the correct order, telling the same story that you have told.

4. Tell a short story aloud using several pictures of key elements or events in the story, presenting each picture as the events occur.   Instruct the student to tell the story once again, using the pictures as memory cues.

5. Ask the students' parents to send you short descriptions of activities done at home the previous day or evening.   The students should attempt to recall the previous evening's activities in correct sequence.   Use leading questions for cues as necessary (e.g., What did you do before dinner?; Did you go anywhere in the car yesterday?). Send home short descriptions of the day's activities at school, asking the parents to do the same activity with the child.

6. Using magazine pictures pasted on paper, ask the student to make up a short descriptive sentence for each picture (e.g., Boys like to play basketball.)   At the end of the session, the student should attempt to recall the sentences he has made up for

each picture. Write the sentences on index cards taped to the back of each picture for checking recall. Use an increasing number of pictures during each subsequent session.

7. Ask the student to get out a pencil and a piece of paper. Give oral directions for activities that can be done with the paper and pencil. For example: Write your name on the back of the paper. Put an x in one corner of the paper. Draw a circle in the center of the paper. Fold the paper in half lengthwise. Place your pencil under the paper.

   The student should attempt to follow the directions in sequence as the number of commands given at one time is gradually increased. To increase the level of difficulty of this task, have the student use a box of crayons and give oral directions employing different colors. For example: Draw a blue triangle on the front of your paper. Draw a green circle on the back of your paper. Draw a black line across your paper, which divides it into two triangles.

8. Using a state or U.S. road map, practice following oral directions. First discuss the map, pointing out major cities, rivers, highways, etc. Then have the student follow a route with a pencil as you present directions aloud. Gradually increase the number of directions presented at one time.

9. Ask the student to give you directions aloud from his house to school, to his grandmother's house, to his father's place of work, etc. You may have to ask the parents to write down some directions to places familiar to the student before beginning this activity.

10. Place 25 common objects in a pile on the table or on the floor in the middle of the room. Place corresponding pictures of the objects arranged in lines in front of the student. As the student watches, place three, four, five or six objects in a bag. Then, ask the student to tell you the order in which the objects were placed in the bag. To supplement this task, you may also wish to have the student order the corresponding pictures of the objects in sequence from left to right in the order in which they were placed in the bag.

11. Use a regular deck of playing cards and remove face cards and aces. After the cards are shuffled, place them face down on the table from the student's left to right as he sits across from you. Begin with a sequence of three, four or five cards, naming the number on the card as you place it face down in front of the student. The student is then asked to repeat the numerical sequence in correct order, flipping the cards over in sequence from left to right to determine if his answer is correct.

12. Provide ten noisemakers (bells, drum, horn, cymbal, etc.) and the corresponding picture for each. Place the pictures in front of the student. While the student has his eyes closed or his back turned, provide a series of noises (three, four, five or as many as appropriate). Then, ask the student to place the corresponding pictures of the noisemakers in the order in which they were presented, sequencing them from left to right.

13. Have a group of students write personal information items on index cards. Examples of items might be: favorite color, sister's name, place of birth, shoe size, type of car family owns, zodiac sign, etc. The students should have the cards in the same order stacked in front of them as they sit in a circle. The students should then go around the circle in turn, showing the appropriate card and stating the item aloud as each particular item is discussed. Then the students should take turns recalling the items that each student has written on his card. For example, the first student would proceed around the circle attempting to name each person's favorite color. If unable to name the item on a particular student's card, he should be cued by having the other student flip his card over revealing the information. This activity could be done as an individual or team competition, determining which student or team could recall the information with the least number of cues (cards being flipped).

References

Bush, W. J. and Giles, M. T. *Aids to Psycholinguistic Teaching.* Columbus, OH: Charles E. Merrill Publishing Company, 1969.

Colin, D., Fillmer, H. T., Lefcourt, A. and Thompson, N. C. *Our Language Today.* New York, NY: Litton Educational Publishing, Inc., 1970.

Keith, R. L. *Speech and Language Rehabilitation.* Danville, IL: Interstate Printers and Publishers, Inc., 1972.

Kilpatrick, K. and Jones, C. *Therapy Guide for Adults with Language and Speech Disorders: A Selection of Stimulation Materials.* Akron, OH: Visiting Nurse Service of Summit County, 1977.

Novakovich, H. and Zoslow, S. *Target on Language.* Bethesda, MD: Christ Church Child Center, 1973.

Rosner, J. *Helping Children Overcome Learning Difficulties.* New York, NY: Walker and Company, 1979.

Stryker, S. *Speech After Stroke.* Springfield, IL: Charles C. Thomas, 1978.

Turner, D. R. *Miller Analogies Test - 1400 Analogy Questions.* New York, NY: Arco Publishing Company, 1973.

Van Hattum, R. J. *Developmental Language Programming for the Retarded.* Boston, MA: Allyn and Bacon, Inc., 1979.

ANSWER KEY

Question Comprehension

Task A   page 42

1. no
2. yes
3. no
4. yes
5. no
6. no
7. yes
8. no
9. no
10. yes
11. no
12. no
13. yes
14. yes
15. yes
16. no
17. yes
18. yes
19. yes
20. no
21. yes
22. no
23. no
24. yes
25. no
26. no
27. no
28. yes
29. yes
30. no
31. no
32. no
33. no
34. yes
35. no
36. no
37. yes
38. yes
39. yes
40. yes
41. no
42. yes
43. no
44. yes
45. no
46. no
47. no
48. no
49. no
50. no
51. no
52. yes
53. no
54. no
55. yes
56. no
57. yes
58. yes
59. no
60. no
61. no
62. no
63. no
64. yes
65. no
66. no
67. yes
68. yes
69. no
70. yes
71. yes

72. no
73. no
74. no
75. yes
76. no
77. yes
78. yes
79. yes
80. yes

Task B   page 45

1. yes
2. no
3. yes
4. yes
5. no
6. no
7. no
8. no
9. no
10. no
11. yes
12. yes
13. no
14. no
15. no
16. no
17. no
18. no
19. no
20. yes
21. yes
22. yes
23. no
24. no
25. yes
26. yes
27. yes
28. yes
29. yes
30. no
31. no
32. yes
33. yes
34. no
35. yes
36. yes
37. yes
38. yes
39. yes
40. no
41. yes
42. yes
43. no
44. no
45. yes
46. no
47. yes
48. yes
49. yes
50. yes
51. no
52. no
53. no
54. yes
55. yes
56. no
57. no
58. yes
59. no
60. yes
61. yes
62. yes
63. yes

64. yes
65. no
66. yes
67. yes
68. yes
69. yes
70. yes
71. yes
72. yes
73. no
74. yes
75. yes
76. yes
77. yes
78. no
79. yes
80. yes

Task C   page 48

1. yes
2. no
3. yes
4. yes
5. yes
6. no
7. no
8. no
9. yes
10. yes
11. yes
12. no
13. yes
14. no
15. yes
16. no
17. no
18. yes
19. yes
20. yes
21. yes
22. yes
23. no
24. yes
25. yes
26. yes
27. no
28. yes
29. no
30. no
31. yes
32. no
33. no
34. yes
35. no
36. yes
37. no
38. no
39. no
40. yes
41. no
42. yes
43. no
44. no
45. no
46. yes
47. yes
48. no
49. no
50. no
51. yes
52. no
53. yes
54. no
55. yes

56. yes
57. yes
58. yes
59. yes
60. yes
61. no
62. no
63. no
64. no
65. no
66. yes
67. no
68. yes
69. yes
70. no
71. yes
72. yes
73. no
74. yes
75. yes
76. yes
77. no
78. yes
79. yes
80. yes

Task D   page 52

1. yes
2. yes
3. no
4. yes
5. yes
6. yes
7. no
8. yes
9. no
10. no
11. no
12. yes
13. yes
14. no
15. no
16. no
17. no
18. yes
19. yes
20. yes
21. yes
22. no
23. yes
24. no
25. yes
26. yes
27. no
28. yes
29. yes
30. yes
31. no
32. yes
33. yes
34. yes
35. no
36. yes
37. no
38. yes
39. no
40. yes
41. no
42. yes
43. no
44. no
45. yes
46. yes
47. yes

ANSWER KEY

48. yes
49. yes
50. yes

Task E   page 54

1. yes
2. no
3. yes
4. yes
5. no
6. no
7. no
8. yes
9. yes
10. no
11. no
12. no
13. yes
14. no
15. yes
16. yes
17. yes
18. no
19. yes
20. yes
21. yes
22. yes
23. yes
24. yes
25. no
26. yes
27. no
28. yes
29. yes
30. yes
31. yes
32. yes
33. yes
34. no
35. no
36. yes
37. yes
38. no
39. yes
40. no
41. yes
42. yes
43. yes
44. no
45. yes
46. no
47. yes
48. no
49. no
50. no
51. yes
52. yes
53. no
54. no
55. no
56. no
57. no
58. yes
59. no
60. yes
61. yes
62. no
63. yes
64. yes
65. no
66. no
67. yes
68. yes
69. no

70. yes
71. no
72. no
73. yes
74. yes
75. yes
76. yes
77. yes
78. no
79. yes
80. yes
81. yes
82. yes
83. yes
84. yes
85. yes
86. yes
87. yes
88. yes
89. no
90. yes
91. yes
92. yes
93. yes
94. yes
95. yes
96. no
97. yes
98. yes
99. yes
100. yes

Task F   page 56

1. yes
2. no
3. yes
4. no
5. yes
6. no
7. no
8. yes
9. no
10. yes
11. yes
12. no
13. no
14. no
15. yes
16. no
17. no
18. no
19. yes
20. no
21. no
22. no
23. yes
24. yes
25. no
26. yes
27. yes
28. yes
29. no
30. no
31. no
32. yes
33. no
34. yes
35. no

Task G   page 57

1. no
2. yes
3. no

4. yes
5. yes
6. no
7. yes
8. no
9. no
10. yes
11. yes
12. no
13. yes
14. no
15. no
16. yes
17. no
18. no
19. no
20. no
21. no
22. yes
23. yes
24. yes
25. yes
26. yes
27. no
28. yes
29. yes
30. yes

Task H   page 59

1. all
2. all
3. some
4. some
5. some
6. all
7. some
8. all
9. some
10. some
11. some
12. some
13. some
14. all
15. all
16. all
17. all
18. some
19. some
20. some
21. some
22. all
23. some
24. some
25. some
26. all
27. some
28. all
29. all
30. some
31. some
32. all
33. some
34. all
35. all
36. some
37. some
38. some
39. all
40. all
41. some
42. some
43. some
44. all
45. some

46. some
47. some
48. some
49. some
50. some
51. some
52. all
53. some
54. some
55. all
56. all
57. all
58. all
59. some
60. all
61. all
62. some
63. all
64. all
65. some
66. all
67. some
68. all
69. all
70. some
71. all
72. all
73. some
74. all
75. all
76. all
77. all
78. all
79. some
80. all

Task I   page 62

1. false
2. false
3. true
4. true
5. true
6. false
7. true
8. true
9. true
10. true
11. false
12. true
13. false
14. true
15. true
16. true
17. true
18. true
19. true
20. true
21. false
22. false
23. true
24. false
25. true
26. false
27. true
28. true
29. false
30. true
31. false
32. true
33. false
34. false
35. true
36. true
37. false

158

ANSWER KEY

38. true
39. true
40. true
41. false
42. false
43. true
44. true
45. false
46. false
47. false
48. true
49. true
50. false

Task J   page 64

1. always
2. sometimes
3. sometimes
4. sometimes
5. always
6. always
7. always
8. sometimes
9. sometimes
10. always
11. sometimes
12. never
13. sometimes
14. never
15. never
16. always
17. sometimes
18. always
19. sometimes
20. always
21. always
22. sometimes
23. never
24. always
25. sometimes
26. sometimes
27. always
28. sometimes
29. sometimes
30. never
31. sometimes
32. always
33. sometimes
34. never
35. always
36. sometimes
37. always
38. never
39. sometimes
40. always
41. always
42. always
43. always
44. always
45. always
46. sometimes
47. sometimes
48. never
49. never
50. always
51. sometimes
52. always
53. never
54. sometimes
55. sometimes
56. always
57. sometimes
58. sometimes
59. sometimes

60. sometimes
61. always
62. always
63. sometimes
64. sometimes
65. always
66. always
67. always
68. sometimes
69. always
70. always
71. sometimes
72. sometimes
73. always
74. sometimes
75. always
76. always
77. sometimes
78. always
79. never
80. never

Association

Task A   page 73

1. it will bleed
2. turn on the light
3. you will get cold
4. you might get hurt
5. you couldn't wear it
6. say hello to him
7. go to sleep
8. turn on the heat
9. you will get wet
10. take them off
11. find a police officer
12. you will be full
13. clean it up
14. they may keep it
15. look it up
16. have a party
17. wait for it to cool
18. you will run out
19. your teacher will be disappointed
20. they will die
21. call them up and ask them
22. the food will spoil
23. the air will go out
24. you are sick
25. they might get washed
26. it will be returned to you
27. have it repaired
28. the cake will stick
29. return it to the store
30. it might cause an accident
31. ring the alarm
32. ask someone for change
33. his team scores
34. return it for the correct size
35. the pictures will be ruined
36. the clothes will not get clean
37. look it up in a dictionary
38. you might get sunburned
39. it must be shot
40. it needs to be wound
41. you forgot to add an ingredient
42. you will be late arriving
43. you will not get any more issues

44. February will have 29 days
45. the sun will not be seen
46. the river is rising
47. you might bounce a check
48. you will be subject to a fine
49. ask a banker
50. ask a broker

Task B   page 75

1. The balloon burst.
2. You may have an accident.
3. The cake was burned.
4. I broke my arm.
5. The neighbor went out.
6. The power went off.
7. an earthquake
8. You may fall down.
9. The chair will break.
10. The records will warp.
11. at the movie
12. I had a nightmare.
13. The washing machine will overflow with suds.
14. The curtains caught on fire.
15. The car will roll down the hill.
16. It was snowing.
17. They had been robbed.
18. The boy had done something wrong.
19. Mark will not be prepared for his speech.
20. The red team won.
21. Halloween
22. It had died.
23. The money was not there.
24. All the food spoiled/ melted.
25. The water boiled away and the pan was burned.
26. It sank.
27. The papers became stuck together.
28. The bathtub overflowed.
29. He did not take any shirts on his trip.
30. a double exposure/a ruined picture

Task D   page 80

1. Go outside now.
2. I was the last one in line.
3. The man is very fat.
4. Raise your right hand.
5. The grapes taste sweet.
6. The sweater is too tight.
7. The cookie jar is full.
8. The ice is rough today.
9. Yesterday, I was early for school.
10. That train is very quiet.
11. Is the box light?
12. That hammock looks very strong.
13. Straight trees are on either side of the road.
14. The football field is small.
15. I arrived home at two o'clock.

16. I bought four boxes of cookies.
17. Your answer is correct.
18. This problem is easy.
19. We export a lot of food.
20. They frequently visit our neighborhood.
21. The towel is dry and hard.
22. The rabbit was slow and dumb.
23. The poor man drove an old car.
24. The pencil is short and dull.
25. New songs are the worst songs.
26. Can you go under the high fence?
27. Light pans cost the least.
28. The bracelet is new and shiny.
29. The boy's skin was very rough.
30. The straight road was heavily traveled.
31. The small dog was very gentle.
32. The old dress is very plain.
33. He missed the baseball on his first try.
34. I was asleep after the snow-storm.
35. Enemies are deceitful.
36. The girl who sits in back of me is skinny.
37. I said goodbye to the first boy in line.
38. Late in the night/evening the house is quiet.
39. We could see the light sky above us as we flew under.
40. The woman's husband is my uncle.

Task E   page 82

1. Always put on your underwear before your jeans.
2. The car is almost out of gas; please stop at the gas station.
3. I took a shower and then I got dried.
4. When I dropped the carton of eggs, the shells broke.
5. The dentist told me that I should brush my teeth daily.
6. The ice cream melted in the hot sun.
7. Last week at school, the teacher assigned us a lot of homework.
8. Grandparents can't watch television without their glasses.
9. In the fall the leaves fall off the trees.
10. I stubbed my toe because I was wearing my sandals.
11. The boys were able to see the baseball game with their binoculars.

12. Mark put in a new light bulb which made the room light.
13. The police officer blew his whistle to stop the traffic.
14. At the swimming pool, there is a lifeguard's chair and a diving board.
15. Mr. Stewart asked the gas station attendant to check under the hood.
16. The hardware store was out of nails.
17. The football team won the game by scoring ten touchdowns.
18. When the light bulb burned out, I replaced it.
19. Because I used suntan lotion, I didn't get a sunburn.
20. The new radiators were working well, putting out hot air.
21. The typewriter typed from left to right.
22. The club elected Sam as their president.
23. The artist thins his paints with turpentine.
24. Last week, I saw a penny fall down the grate.
25. The building fell down because it was old.
26. The ball bounced down the steps and rolled out the door.
27. Our church has 25 people singing in the choir.
28. The hockey player was benched for throwing his stick at a player.
29. The mother of the bride was so happy she cried during the entire wedding.
30. The fire was not hot enough, so I threw some more wood on it.

Task F page 84

Accept
appropriate
responses.

Task G page 87

I.

1. bee, mouse, rabbit
2. rope, cage, net
3. whistle, cricket, alarm clock
4. paper, bag. fingernail
5. wax, plastic, crayon
6. poster, cloud
7. log, ship
8. snake, bicycle, wind, river
9. bowling ball, tire, planet
10. stick, plate, person's leg, balloon
11. elbow, rubber band, tree
12. door, tape, stamp
13. airplane, balloon, kite

14. savings account, moss, hair, fingernails
15. rolling pin, dog, tide

II.

1. mouth, book
2. shoes, penny
3. gum, tobacco
4. boat, board
5. paint, gasoline
6. glass, paper bag
7. hand, animal
8. fan, mixer
9. hands, arms
10. thunder, the wind
11. star, cloud
12. perfume, shampoo
13. radio, fan
14. waxed floor, banana peel
15. clock, motor
16. lawn, hair
17. teeth, paint
18. paper plate, water hose
19. electric razor, pain
20. cold, train

Task H page 89

1. song
2. ouch
3. pinch
4. teacher
5. slow
6. night
7. skunk
8. grape
9. seam
10. rough
11. tear
12. court
13. dock
14. graze
15. borrow
16. huddle
17. plow
18. marriage
19. trace
20. share
21. cheat
22. calm
23. pro
24. tax
25. plugs

Task I page 90

1. airplane, airport, airway, airborne, aircraft
2. sailboat, boatload, boat house, rowboat, lifeboat
3. sunshine, sundown, sunburn, sunfish, sunflower
4. schoolboy, schoolmate, schoolhouse, schoolroom
5. sandbox, sandblast, sandbag, sandman, sandpaper
6. doorbell, doorway, doorstop, doorman, doorknob
7. school yard, lumberyard, yardstick, yardarm

8. lifeguard, lifeboat, lifelike, Lifesaver, lifetime
9. bedside, bedroom, sickbed, bedtime, bedspread
10. eyelash, eyeball, eyebrow, eyesore, eyewitness
11. checkbook, checkmate, checkout, checkroom, hatcheck
12. bookcase, bookmark, bookmaker, bookbinder, bookmobile
13. raindrop, rainfall, rainbow, raincoat, rainstorm
14. keyhole, keystone, keynote, turnkey, keyboard
15. shoelace, shoemaker, shoeshine, shoestring, horseshoe
16. gunrack, gun-shy, gunfire, shotgun, gunpowder
17. goldfish, fishbowl, fish pond, fish hook, bluefish
18. moonlight, moonshine, moonlit, moonbeam, moonstruck
19. nosegay, nose guard, nose-dive, bluenose, nosebleed
20. bullfrog, bullfinch, bullfight, bulldozer, bulldog
21. shipboard, shipmate, shipwreck, shipyard, shipman
22. grandfather, godfather, forefather, stepfather
23. mankind, mailman, fireman, manpower, manhole
24. football, footstep, tenderfoot, footstool, footwork
25. bagboy, bookbag, bagpipe, shoe bag, windbag
26. nightmare, nightgown, nightcap, nightfall, nightshirt
27. hairbrush, haircut, hairpin, hairpiece, horsehair
28. handwriting, handcuff, second-hand, handbag
29. buckshot, buckskin, buckeye, buckwheat
30. grandfather, grandchild, grandson, grandstand, grandmother

Task J page 91

I.

1. dog
2. duck
3. cat
4. bird
5. bee
6. cow
7. pig
8. lion
9. horse
10. bear
11. bird

12. owl
13. chicken
14. mosquito, gnat
15. sheep
16. dove, pigeon
17. coyote, wolf
18. frog
19. crow
20. pig
21. rooster
22. monkey
23. sheep
24. donkey
25. cattle

II.

1. fish
2. bird
3. bee
4. rabbit, kangaroo
5. horse
6. chicken, woodpecker
7. bug, snake
8. bronco
9. snake
10. horse
11. cow
12. bee
13. bird, chicken
14. duck
15. bird, snake
16. bear
17. snake
18. eagle
19. pig
20. rabbit, mole

III.

1. ball
2. knife, scissors
3. glass
4. boat, chair
5. balloon, bubble
6. gun
7. sun, light
8. water, faucet
9. ice cream
10. person, motor
11. bell
12. boat
13. nose, skunk
14. paper
15. ball
16. fire
17. water, freezer
18. wind
19. stove
20. door
21. picture, clothes
22. top
23. paper
24. soap
25. door
26. flower
27. hammer
28. sweater, elastic
29. river
30. boat
31. a leg, wire
32. rock
33. tree
34. firecracker
35. page, car

36. clothes
37. eggshell
38. traffic light
39. blood, grass
40. bolt, preacher
41. volcano
42. electricity
43. pancake
44. needle
45. door, glue
46. iron
47. bell
48. eye
49. prices
50. story
51. drink
52. car
53. fence
54. heat
55. sponge
56. beam
57. balloon
58. gear
59. car
60. bridge
61. noise
62. water
63. match
64. plow
65. record
66. light
67. temperature
68. bell
69. sail
70. log

Task K   page 94

I.

1. cry or cries
2. fights
3. marches, shouts
4. cuts
5. paints
6. dances
7. cooks
8. fixes
9. flies
10. plants
11. helps, directs
12. cleans
13. drills
14. acts
15. heals
16. preaches
17. serves
18. plays, entertains
19. drives
20. types
21. sews
22. builds
23. teaches
24. designs
25. rules
26. rides
27. carries
28. defends
29. legislates
30. commands

II.

1. opens
2. cuts

3. cooks
4. bounces
5. flies
6. turns, cools
7. rings
8. writes
9. colors
10. rings
11. blows
12. blooms
13. cleans
14. sticks
15. cuts, mows
16. sails
17. sews
18. weighs
19. dries
20. ticks
21. beats
22. plows
23. burns, melts
24. shaves
25. turns, tightens
26. heals
27. magnifies
28. protects
29. amplifies
30. swings

Task L   page 96

1. elephant
   bear
   bear
   elephant
   elephant
2. tree
   tree
   flower
   flower
   tree
3. lake
   ocean
   ocean
   ocean
   lake
4. pizza
   chocolate cake
   pizza
   chocolate cake
   pizza
5. table
   table
   rocking chair
   table
   table
6. drum
   bugle
   bugle
   drum
   bugle
7. book
   book
   magazine
   book
   magazine
8. jeans
   jeans
   sweater
   jeans
   jeans

9. pencil
   pencil
   pen
   pen
   pen
10. potato
    apple
    apple
    potato
    potato

Task M   page 99

I.

1. house
   lion
   bicycle
   canoe
   chain
2. ice
   Popsicle
   lemonade
   pool
   snow
3. siren
   scream
   train
   tap shoes
   earthquake
4. leg
   belt
   football field
   pencil
   yardstick
5. bear
   cage
   banana peel
   rope
   metal
6. draw a circle
   cook a hot dog
   dial a telephone
   go to a party
   scrub the floor
7. bed
   table
   pie
   pencil
   brick
8. knife
   saw
   pencil
   tooth
   ice skates
9. thumb
   slice of toast
   whipped cream
   yarn
   dictionary
10. fur coat
    skateboard
    television
    airplane
    china plate

II.

1. butterfly
2. hands
3. clown
4. witch
5. circus
6. an ice cream cone
7. kitten

8. man
9. someone with the flu
10. glue
11. grandparent
12. pillow
13. ghost
14. towel
15. water
16. house
17. toy spider
18. cabin
19. knee
20. bike
21. bee
22. sleeping bag
23. wall
24. toaster
25. spatula

III.

1. ice cream
2. stove
3. stamp
4. chair
5. boy
6. tree
7. jet
8. Coke
9. knife
10. party dress
11. meat
12. potato chip
13. London
14. sand
15. gum
16. ant
17. slice of bread
18. puddle
19. mirror
20. coat
21. Autumn leaves
22. plastic jug
23. pantyhose
24. computer
25. priest

IV.

1. envelope
2. midnight
3. pretzels
4. corn chip
5. library
6. adult
7. ice
8. bobcat
9. movie
10. taffy
11. broken leg
12. burlap
13. toast
14. pig
15. kitten
16. soap
17. rain
18. leopard
19. rollercoaster
20. green beans

Task N   page 104

1. toys
2. steering wheel, tire
3. car, truck
4. paper

ANSWER KEY

5. television
6. bed
7. sun, moon
8. telephone
9. square, rectangle
10. book, door
11. fan
12. wallet, bank
13. cup, can
14. soap
15. escalator, elevator
16. window
17. kitchen
18. ashtray
19. dictionary
20. hive
21. hydrant
22. corner
23. globe
24. flock
25. suds, lather
26. lasso
27. atlas
28. telescope
29. hurricane
30. fraternity
31. antique
32. census
33. jack
34. notary
35. shingle

Task O   page 106

1. shoes, feet, pair
2. man, cold, winter
3. water, box, bubble
4. nail, pound, build
5. cry, diapers, boy/girl
6. shine, hot, burn
7. play, toy, baby
8. sit, table, rocking
9. class, homework, desk
10. coffee, saucer, glass
11. spoon, cut, sharp
12. toast, bake, sandwich
13. nest, fly, robin
14. tie, cold, jacket
15. milk, barn, moo
16. light, shade, bulb
17. door, key, combination
18. pop, baby, cork
19. cut, lawn mower, green
20. ink, pencil, write
21. glass, curtain, door
22. window, room, door
23. needle, sew, stitch
24. cigarette, fire, pipe
25. bed, slippers, robe
26. deliver, mail, alphabet
27. clothes, heavy, grip
28. hot, sand, camel
29. expensive, jewelry, mine
30. money, time, save
31. animal, free, crazy
32. under, shoe, easy
33. no, sir, man
34. bell, finger, around
35. vinegar, machinery, slick
36. Army, parade, demonstration
37. celebrate, family, food
38. member, dues, weapon
39. crop, water, factory
40. sleep, land, nightmare

41. shoe, apple, repairman
42. beach, stone, little
43. paint, artist, stand
44. float, drift, beach
45. coat, shoes, broom
46. outer, room, ship
47. shape, duplicate, paper
48. tree, fruit, apple
49. borrow, money, debt
50. venetian, eyes, fold

Task P   page 107

1. opposite
2. opposite
3. same
4. opposite
5. opposite
6. opposite
7. opposite
8. same
9. same
10. opposite
11. opposite
12. opposite
13. same
14. opposite
15. opposite
16. same
17. same
18. same
19. opposite
20. opposite
21. opposite
22. same
23. opposite
24. same
25. opposite
26. same
27. opposite
28. same
29. same
30. same
31. same
32. opposite
33. same
34. opposite
35. same
36. same
37. opposite
38. same
39. opposite
40. opposite
41. opposite
42. same
43. same
44. same
45. opposite
46. same
47. same
48. same
49. opposite
50. same
51. opposite
52. opposite
53. same
54. same
55. opposite
56. same
57. same
58. same
59. opposite
60. opposite
61. opposite
62. opposite

63. same
64. same
65. opposite
66. same
67. same
68. same
69. same
70. opposite
71. opposite
72. same
73. same
74. opposite
75. same
76. same
77. same
78. opposite
79. same
80. opposite
81. same
82. same
83. opposite
84. opposite
85. same
86. opposite
87. same
88. opposite
89. same
90. same
91. same
92. opposite
93. same
94. same
95. opposite
96. opposite
97. same
98. opposite
99. opposite
100. same
101. opposite
102. same
103. same
104. opposite
105. same
106. same
107. opposite
108. opposite
109. same
110. opposite
111. same
112. same
113. same
114. same
115. opposite
116. same
117. same
118. same
119. opposite
120. same

Task Q   page 109

1. down
2. go
3. out
4. little
5. bad
6. day
7. hard
8. girl
9. sad
10. skinny
11. outside
12. father
13. fast
14. shut

15. short
16. cold
17. new
18. dry
19. right
20. under
21. white
22. hard
23. soft
24. found
25. dark
26. smooth
27. short
28. near
29. curly
30. awake
31. woman
32. adult
33. old
34. light
35. mean
36. low
37. sour
38. last
39. good-bye
40. wrong
41. miss
42. well
43. late
44. poor
45. top
46. evening
47. loser
48. weak
49. pull
50. many
51. yours
52. deep
53. below
54. end
55. throw
56. hate
57. his
58. take
59. false
60. dull
61. ugly
62. finish
63. easy
64. friend
65. lose
66. answer
67. divorce
68. lead
69. failure
70. hell
71. sell
72. spend
73. scream
74. basement
75. wide
76. male
77. forget
78. present
79. sink
80. polite
81. nephew
82. peace
83. floor
84. you
85. careless
86. death
87. learn
88. toe
89. past

ANSWER KEY

90. divide
91. fictional
92. con
93. subtract
94. seek
95. stallion
96. hen
97. colt
98. valley
99. worst
100. sweet
101. ignorant
102. clumsy
103. advance
104. guilty
105. busy
106. omit
107. hero
108. defense
109. exhale
110. solo
111. punishment
112. defeat
113. never
114. freedom
115. decrease
116. solid
117. amateur
118. poverty
119. real
120. plentiful
121. longitude
122. avoid
123. permanent
124. discourage
125. capture
126. destroy
127. deny
128. credit
129. pursue
130. mobile
131. collect
132. liberal
133. safe
134. depart
135. accept
136. hope
137. extinguish
138. decelerate
139. reveal
140. conclude
141. cooperative
142. foreigner
143. frugal
144. repel
145. acquit
146. conclusion
147. withdraw
148. motorist
149. expert
150. darken

Task R   page 112

1. unclean
2. unsafe
3. dishonest
4. distrust
5. unhappy
6. unsure
7. incorrect
8. illegal
9. unlock
10. disagree
11. undress
12. unbutton
13. unzip
14. disobey
15. uncertain
16. unimportant
17. unfriendly
18. imperfect
19. unclear
20. disapprove
21. insane
22. inexpensive
23. non-fiction
24. umemployment
25. immodest
26. unsanitary
27. discontinue
28. uncurl
29. immature
30. impure
31. disloyal
32. discontent
33. disinterest
34. inexperienced
35. inflexible
36. immobile
37. ineffective
38. unsteady
39. immoderate
40. non-negotiable
41. undesirable
42. uncooperative
43. irregular
44. irreverent
45. irrelevant
46. irreversible
47. untame
48. insufficient
49. impartial
50. inflammable

Task S   page 114

1. girl
2. down
3. little
4. cold
5. hard
6. sick
7. good-bye
8. outside
9. fast
10. awake
11. stop
12. young
13. summer
14. poor
15. skinny
16. dry
17. absent
18. sweet
19. above
20. smooth
21. empty
22. under
23. short
24. female
25. deep
26. different
27. subtract
28. graceful
29. safe
30. inexpensive
31. sell
32. late
33. false
34. solo
35. destroy
36. mature
37. non-fictional
38. real
39. finite
40. solid
41. plentiful
42. con
43. innocent
44. punishment
45. stallion
46. retreat
47. conclude
48. pedestrian
49. expert
50. foreigner

Task T   page 117

1. apples
2. seeing
3. paws
4. arm
5. writing, clapping
6. ring
7. yellow
8. petals
9. locks, knobs
10. zippers
11. strings
12. engine
13. fur
14. claws
15. three
16. wires
17. rectangular
18. erasers
19. students
20. letters
21. wicks
22. desks
23. burrow, hole
24. curtain
25. days
26. wrenches
27. trunks
28. chins
29. home plates
30. negatives
31. cold
32. dinner
33. drink
34. water
35. day
36. eat
37. husband
38. feet
39. ears
40. chalkboard
41. meow
42. bed
43. jar
44. caution, wait
45. floor
46. roll
47. letter
48. birds
49. head
50. meat
51. quack
52. day
53. fish
54. sweet
55. princess
56. old
57. fisherman
58. fish
59. ship
60. fruit
61. full
62. television
63. sad
64. neck
65. horse
66. track
67. spaceships
68. sad
69. end
70. bathroom
71. toes
72. court
73. book
74. bread
75. December
76. valley
77. doctor
78. honey
79. nails
80. shirt
81. green, purple
82. terminal
83. grass
84. niece
85. bird
86. grow
87. vegetable
88. Florida
89. hour
90. pancake
91. electricity
92. football game
93. orchestra, train
94. cutting
95. frog
96. navy
97. foot
98. couch, chair
99. Greece
100. balloon

1-3-123457